"*Writing the Intimate Character*, the latest engaging guide by Jordan Rosenfeld, is a rich resource we'll all be learning from for the rest of our lives. 'Does the term point of view seem too dull and dry?' she asks. 'Try intimacy instead.' And then she shows us how, with diverse examples and wise observation. Now that I have Jordan's take on how to create a character from the inside out, I'm eager to get to it. You, too, will find this book that inspiring."

—REBECCA LAWTON, AUTHOR OF *SACRAMENT: HOMAGE TO A RIVER* AND OTHER BOOKS

....

"*Writing the Intimate Character* provides insights, examples, and exercises that will be useful not only to those who are new to writing fiction but to those, like myself, who are coming back to it after a break. Jordan Rosenfeld's explanation of how narrative voice works with point of view and other literary elements to create characters that readers care deeply about is clear and revelatory. The book can be worked through methodically or dipped into as needed. It's a useful tool for getting the gears of imagination working or for jump-starting and fine-tuning a work in process."

—ZOE ZOLBROD, AUTHOR OF THE NOVEL *CURRENCY* AND THE MEMOIR *THE TELLING*

....

"Jordan Rosenfeld has a keen insight into how to construct characters who are truly lived-in. With intelligence and wit, she walks you through every element of powerful characterization, from selecting your POV to demonstrating character growth throughout your story. Whether you're new to fiction or a more experienced writer, put your trust in Jordan Rosenfeld; she'll help you tell a better story."

—LAURA BOGART, FREELANCE WRITER AND NOVELIST

WRITING
the intimate
CHARACTER

WRITER'S DIGEST
BOOKS

WritersDigest.*com*
Cincinnati, Ohio

WRITING THE INTIMATE CHARACTER. Copyright © 2016 by Jordan Rosenfeld. Manufactured in the United States of America. All rights reserved. No other part of this book may be reproduced in any form or by any electronic or mechanical means, including information storage and retrieval systems, without permission in writing from the publisher, except by a reviewer, who may quote brief passages in a review. Published by Writer's Digest Books, an imprint of F+W Media, Inc., 10151 Carver Road, Cincinnati, Ohio 45242. (800) 289-0963.

For more resources for writers, visit www.writersdigest.com.

20 19 18 17 16   5 4 3 2 1

Distributed in Canada by Fraser Direct
100 Armstrong Avenue
Georgetown, Ontario, Canada L7G 5S4
Tel: (905) 877-4411

Distributed in the U.K. and Europe by F+W Media International
Brunel House, Newton Abbot, Devon, TQ12 4PU, England
Tel: (+44) 1626-323200, Fax: (+44) 1626-323319
E-mail: postmaster@davidandcharles.co.ukLibrary of Congress Cataloging-in-Publication Data

ISBN-13: 978-1-4403-4602-6

Edited by Rachel Randall
Designed by Alexis Estoye
Production coordinated by Debbie Thomas

DEDICATION

To all of my editors, who have firmly and lovingly shaped my words for public consumption

ACKNOWLEDGMENTS

Any time I write a book, I must thank my family and friends for their patience with me, for being patient in the face of all the social activities I declined and the time I spent huddled over my computer. Specifically, though, I wonder how I survived writing before I met Amy McElroy, who holds my hand when I'm breaking down, offers suggestions, talks me off ledges and onto the spin bike—no questions asked. I'm also deeply grateful to Dawn Carr, whose own burning-hot drive for knowledge and steady support makes me think that being obsessed with writing is not so crazy after all. And, of course, the rest of my bitches, who know who they are, thus named because they put up with all of my bitchin'. And, most important, to all the writers whose books shaped, moved, and formed me, and taught me everything I know about writing, and to the mentors and teachers who helped me translate that into an understanding of craft.

ABOUT THE AUTHOR

Jordan Rosenfeld is the author of the writing guides *Writing Deep Scenes: Plotting Your Story Through Action, Emotion, and Theme*, with Martha Alderson; *A Writer's Guide to Persistence: How to Create a Lasting and Productive Writing Practice*; *Make a Scene: Crafting a Powerful Story One Scene at a Time*; and *Write Free: Attracting the Creative Life*, with Rebecca Lawton. She is also the author of the suspense novels *Women in Red*, *Forged in Grace*, and *Night Oracle*.

Jordan's articles and essays have been published in such places as *The Atlantic*, *The Daily Beast*, *LitHub*, *mental_floss*, *The New York Times*, *Ozy*, *Pacific Standard*, *Quartz*, Salon.com, *The Washington Post*, *Writer's Digest*, *The Writer*, and more. Visit her website, www.jordan rosenfeld.net, or follow her on Twitter @JordanRosenfeld.

TABLE *of* CONTENTS

PART THREE
Stretch Your Skills

INTRODUCTION

Think for a moment about your favorite novels. These are the books you can't put down, the ones you force yourself to keep reading well into the wee hours of the morning, until your eyelids are sandy and your brain is buzzing with excitement and exhaustion. What makes these stories so compelling, so engaging, so … un-put-downable?

The answer, in a word: *characters*. Unforgettable, vivid, chatty, bold, wild, foolish, singular characters that are so authentic, so true and real, that you feel as if you're living in their world—or, even better, *inside* of them. And while it may not be obvious to the *reader*, the main mechanism writers can use to deeply engage with characters is *point of view*. Strong point of view creates a powerful, sensory experience that draws readers into your characters' inner landscape and confidently directs your audience to the story you're trying to tell. When the masterful use of point of view is applied to a story, it won't just *tell* readers about an experience; it will allow them to *live* it through a character.

Does the term *point of view* seem too dry and dull? Try *intimacy* instead. It's a much sexier word, isn't it? The best stories offer a deeply intimate experience. When thinking about character intimacy, ask yourself: How close do you want your readers to be to your story? Do you want them to be distant observers, or do you want them to slip right into the skin of your protagonist? Learn to master point of view—or the level of intimacy through which you share your characters' experiences—and you will do more than capture readers' minds and hearts. You'll merge them with your characters. The result will be a book that readers won't be able to resist.

Writing the Intimate Character eschews the dull, didactic explanations of point of view so commonly found in other writing texts. Instead you'll discover a point-of-view system based on character cues: specific behaviors, sensory perceptions, dialogue, and visual imagery. Point of view is the lens through which the reader experiences your characters' emotions and thoughts. You'll learn how character emotions manifest on two distinct levels: as *surface feelings* and as *subset feelings*. These levels allow you to dive deeply to build richer, more fully rounded characters. We'll also talk about how to weave thoughts (internal monologue) and emotion together with action.

We'll look at every element of a story, from exposition to interior monologue to plot, through the lens of point of view, while studying examples from best-selling literature. Throughout the book I offer exercises so you can test-drive each point of view for your own work. These tools and techniques will help you create a multisensory, layered emotional experience within your story.

Readers connect with characters whose senses they can experience, whose minds they can enter, and whose emotions they can feel. If you want to write characters of this caliber, turn the page.

PART ONE
Character-Building Essentials

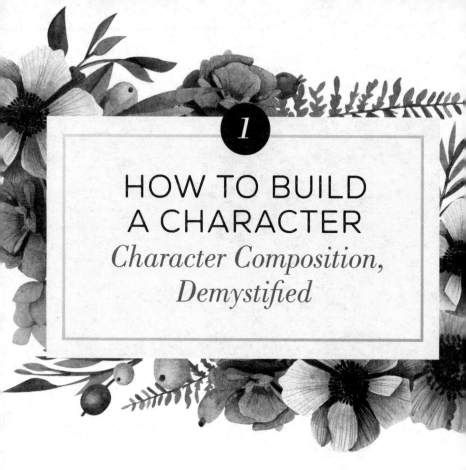

HOW TO BUILD A CHARACTER
Character Composition, Demystified

> *"I have wanted you to see out of my eyes so many times."*

—ELIZABETH BERG, *THE PULL OF THE MOON*

Where do fictional characters come from, and, more important, how do you build one from scratch? For some writers, characters whisper in their ears or appear in their dreams; for others, building a character requires as much effort and forethought as constructing a house. Though the method will vary for every writer, there's no wrong way to build a character. But before you begin fleshing out this imaginary person, it is useful to visualize her as real, vivid, and alive. The more real your character is to you, the more real she will be to readers.

This chapter is a brief recipe for character building, especially if you're not quite sure where or how to start.

PICK A POINT OF VIEW

As much as this is a book about character, it is even more a book about point of view (POV), because you simply can't separate a character from your chosen storytelling method (though you can do so carelessly, which is a habit this book aims to help you correct). To define it simply, POV is two things:

1. It's a storytelling device that allows a reader access to your characters' inner lives (emotions, thoughts, sensory experience).
2. It's the way you share a unique character's worldview and the events he experiences in the world (opinions, philosophy, observations).

Only through POV can a young Caucasian girl in Nebraska learn the perspective of a Native American shaman or peek into the mind of a prisoner who regrets his actions. POV is the magic that helps translate character experiences for readers.

Naturally, it's important to consider the POV you'll use before you begin writing your character, or at least before you get too deep into your draft. This is because POV is also the lens that focuses the story for your reader. Do you want your protagonist to share deeply intimate insights, so that the reader is privy to his every thought? Then you might find that first-person POV fits your needs. Do you need the freedom to roam in and out of multiple POVs and to offer information the characters don't know? You might choose the omniscient POV.

Making an informed decision about your story's POV is also important because you don't want to write one hundred pages of your manuscript and realize that the POV you picked on a whim isn't working for you. Believe me: Speaking from experience, it's no fun to single-handedly change the POV, line by line, for several hundred pages. For that reason, I recommend writing some character sketches or a few test-run chapters in several different POVs. For instance, write a scene in first person in which your character does something that makes her feel guilty. Write another scene in third-person intimate in which she experiences a happiness she's never known before. Try a third scene in the distant and versatile omniscient viewpoint in which she discovers a painful secret.

Once you read through the chapters in Part Two, you'll have a better sense of how POV works, which will allow you to choose the right one for your story.

SELECT A VERB TENSE

Verb tense is a detail many writers forget to consider in advance, but it plays a vital role in determining the intimacy level between characters and readers. *Tense* refers to the conjugation of the verbs in your novel. Nothing interrupts a smooth reading flow faster than inconsistent verb tenses—and you want to make absolutely sure that when you submit your manuscript to an agent or a publisher, you've corrected any inconsistencies.

The two most common verb tenses for fiction are present tense and past tense.

- **PRESENT TENSE:** Verbs are in the *now*: "I go," "he sees," "we touch." This creates immediacy, even urgency. When combined with first-person POV, this tense creates hyperintimacy, a style used most commonly in young adult fiction and more contemporary novels. Some readers say it is "too present"; they prefer the small amount of emotional distance past-tense verbs provide. Depending on how old you are, you may either love this tense or detest it.
- **PAST TENSE:** While these verbs are formatted so that the action is in the past—"I went," "he saw," "we touched"—the story might still take place in the present. Only the verbs themselves differ from their present-tense forms. The past tense puts a little more distance between characters and readers, and softens the sense of immediacy. It's a common and useful tense, and a perfect choice for many books.

CRAFT A FLAWED BUT SYMPATHETIC PERSON

All great fiction introduces us to people who are flawed but sympathetic in some way. A character must be *relatable*: She might mess up or mess around, make bad choices, have a bad temper, speak before she thinks, or forget to file her taxes. And yet she must also be able to elicit *sympathy*; her flaws should be forgivable. They should serve to make the character *human*.

A sympathetic character doesn't have to be a likable one, and he definitely shouldn't be perfect. A "perfect" character is much like a robot: someone without flaws or foibles, who tackles every obstacle without resistance, who never doubts himself or makes mistakes. And reading about a robot isn't compelling or engaging (unless your character is a sentient robot that goes rogue).

"Perfect" characters usually seem annoying, narcissistic, or unstable. Fiction's purpose may be to entertain, but it also helps us connect with difficult aspects of the human condition. It validates and explains the complex array of emotions that color our experiences and our lives. (In fact, researchers at The New School of New York conducted a study, published in the October 2015 issue of the journal *Science*, that revealed that fiction readers show an increased capacity for empathy and for experiencing compassion for people vastly different from themselves.) The more *surmountable* flaws your characters have, the better readers will connect with them.

Here are a few examples of flawed characters who transform their flaws into strengths:

- Katniss Everdeen of The Hunger Games series can be stubborn and self-sacrificing. This flaw eventually translates into honesty and integrity that allow her to speak hard truths and stand up for the underdog.
- Hermione Granger in the Harry Potter books often blurts out information like a know-it-all, but she has the actual knowledge

to back up this flaw, and this trait becomes valuable to dozens of other characters over the course of the books.

Sometimes the character's situation at the beginning is more compelling than the character. For example, think of the kid who is forced by his cruel aunt and uncle to sleep in the cupboard under the stairs, while his cousin is given every comfort. This character has an interesting situation that keeps the reader's attention focused on what happens next. And while we eventually come to love the character of Harry Potter based on his merits and flaws, it is his initial situation that hooks us from the start.

INTRODUCE A PROBLEM

To make a character's life interesting enough to sustain a plot, you need to give her a problem so tremendous that it will force change in her outer life as well as her inner reality. This problem also must be big enough to create ripples of consequence throughout the story. It should elicit conflicting feelings in your protagonist and affect the lives of others. Christopher Vogler, a plot specialist and the author of *The Writer's Mythic Journey*, calls this problem "a call to adventure," but I like to add that it can also be "an unwanted change." Not everything that happens to a character is, at first, a matter of choice. While many characters do choose an adventure, in other instances change is thrust upon them. Think of stories in which a character receives a negative medical diagnosis, suffers the death of a loved one, loses a job, receives divorce papers, or is forced on a quest based on an ancient prophecy. The key to a strong problem is that it forces your protagonist to rise to the challenge, even when she doesn't want to.

Other problems—I think of these as the "bait and switch" variety—involve a character who accepts a call to adventure that turns out to be different from what she expected. Or perhaps the adventure is more complicated than she initially thought.

A story problem must press, test, stretch, and challenge your protagonist, forcing her into the darkest depths of her flaws and into the brightest light of her strengths.

The best stories are those in which the problem is indelibly linked to the character herself. For example, in one of my favorite trilogies by Deborah Harkness, which begins with *A Discovery of Witches*, the protagonist, Diana Bishop, is a modern American witch who refuses to learn how to use her powers because magic, in essence, killed her parents. Unfortunately, magic has other plans for her, and when she unwittingly pulls an enchanted book from Oxford's Bodleian Library, it awakens her magic powers and sends all manner of strange and dangerous creatures—and plot problems—her way. In the first book, the problem is introduced when Diana accesses the magic of the dangerous ancient book. However, this problem arises directly from her own character—her unwillingness to learn magic. If she had honed her magical skills, she would have known how dangerous the book was and what she should have done with it.

Of course, the problem in your story can be grounded in reality rather than fantasy. For example, a character's refusal to consent to an arranged marriage might lead her to escape her home, or a character's choice to pursue his singing career might put him in the midst of a sketchy group of people. There are endless possibilities and problems to choose from.

DISCOVER WHAT HAUNTS YOUR CHARACTER

You've probably seen the term *backstory* in other writing books—most likely with the instruction to avoid using it in your novel. Backstory is the big bag of history that your character carries around with him. It is comprised of all the events that happened to the character prior to the beginning of your story.

We all have a backstory. That cranky teller at the bank has a backstory that probably explains why she's so cranky. But unless you ask her directly or coax it out of her, you'll never know the reason. Instead, you will simply witness the way her backstory informs her behavior. In fiction, the trick is to keep the character's backstory to a minimum.

Allow your character to be haunted by it. Let it drip from your character's seams in a trickle rather than flooding the story with too much detail.

Characters ought to be haunted by something: a childhood loss, a recent breakup, a dream unfulfilled. This is often called a "wound," and it's part of the necessary process of taking a character through a transformation within your story (more on this in chapter twelve). It's very important to think about what this wound might be before your story begins, and as you design your character.

CREATE A HYBRID CHARACTER

If you struggle to cut characters from whole cloth, you may find it much easier to borrow fragments from real people in your life, and even from yourself. Your eccentric sixth-grade science teacher with the lisp might make the perfect basis for a scientist in the novel you're writing. Or that nervous snort your grandfather makes when he's laughing hard might work perfectly as one of your protagonist's traits.

Or maybe you had a series of friends who fit a similar mold over the years—a "type," if you will. Maybe they were all good looking and charismatic, but manipulative. You could pull the "sameness" from them and create a composite character who shares all of these traits, condensing them into one person.

You can also, of course, borrow from yourself. Try giving your character some of the best bits of you, as well as some of your flaws, since you have a virtual encyclopedia of insights and imagery from which to borrow.

When you are inspired by reality, you can access layers of information and sensory imagery compiled from years of experiences. I modeled a character in my novel-in-progress after an extended family member who spoke in big words with a Southern accent. When writing him, I could hear the precise cadence of his voice. I could see the pallor of his skin and the ropy muscles in his calves. I could smell the sweet-rot fug of alcohol that often permeated the air around him, and I could imagine the sorts of things he would say to my other characters. Of course, the fictional version of him was vastly different from the real man, but taking the leap was so much easier when I started with a true-life model.

BORROW FROM TRUE EVENTS AND HISTORY

On a similar note, many writers are inspired by historical figures and tales. Fictional versions of almost every major public figure, politician, and celebrity have appeared in print at the hand of an intrepid writer. You may have a story in mind that derives from a true source, which gives you some parameters to work within. Here are some considerations when fictionalizing a real person:

- **STRIVE FOR AUTHENTICITY.** Research will be required to get authentic details, background, personal life, etc., just right. Study this person's actual words in whatever form they exist. If she is contemporary, study her mannerisms and voice—all the ways she acts and speaks—so you can represent her accurately.
- **SATIRE GRANTS MORE FREEDOM.** You have a legal right to represent a historical person for means of satire, which grants you more freedom from potential legal fallout. Avoid anything that could constitute slander.
- **GET TO KNOW THE CHARACTER'S BIGGEST FEARS AND GREATEST DESIRES.** In all people, fictional or real, these two factors are the most essential for building a character who reads authentically on the page.
- **DETERMINE THE CHARACTER'S ARC.** A historical person might have been involved in any number of story-worthy events, but what is the story *you* wish to tell, and what is your character's arc of change? Start at a point in which he has something to learn but is still working within the framework of unconscious motivations or actions. Tell a story of change.

VISUALIZE YOUR CHARACTER

Being able to "see" your character can be especially important for writers who are visual learners. Using magazine clippings or Photoshop, create a composite image based on how you see your character in your mind's eye. If you happen to have a celebrity in mind who can stand in for your character, use her image to help you include more realistic details in your writing. Readers need to be able to see your character as vividly as if they were standing in the room, and the only way to do this is if you have drawn authentically on all the senses to paint a portrait. (You get bonus points if your character becomes so real in your mind that you think you spot her in a crowd!) At the same time, avoid generalizations and clichés—no "medium height," "ice-blue eyes," "glistening locks," or descriptions of her as "petite."

Here's a quick character description from Tom Spanbauer's literary novel, *I Loved You More*. The protagonist, Ben, slips into a writing workshop with a famous, egotistical writer named Hank, with whom he quickly falls in love. In this scene he focuses on one small, telling detail about himself that sets the stage for how he feels in contrast to Hank.

> Then I notice something I wish I'd never noticed. My right sock has a big hole in it and there's my big toe poking out. With green glitter on it. Then there's the smell. Wet socks and sweat from the platform shoes. I'm sure the smell isn't half as bad as I imagine it. But still, the rest of Hank's story, I don't hear a word because all I can think of is the smell coming off my feet.

The sensory description of a smelly sock with a hole in it—what better metaphor for this character's shame? Small details about what he is wearing—the platform shoes, the green glitter—also tell us that the shame Ben is experiencing might have to do with his being gay.

The following passage from Lidia Yuknavitch's novel *The Small Backs of Children* is so full of imagery and music that it is essentially poetry. It is told from the point of view of a character named "The Filmmaker," written in the rare second-person POV.

For the opening, you decided to move in slow motion and black-and-white. An excruciatingly beautiful girl gone to woman, walking. A girl who has toppled over into woman, her lips already in a pout between yes and no, her torso and ass breaking faith. Moving down a tree-lined city sidewalk. Fall. Her coat pulled up to the flush of her cheeks. Her hands stuffed down into pockets. Her hair making art in the wind.

Yuknavitch artfully puts the reader in the point of view of a filmmaker, showing us this character as though we are watching her onscreen. Her descriptions are not literal—what does a "girl who has toppled over into woman" actually look like, for instance? And yet the metaphor makes no bones about what it means; you can visualize a young girl becoming a woman, perhaps in a haphazard way.

These examples should help you think beyond the obvious "what does my character look like?" descriptions and explore nuances such as:

- What is your character's gait like? Does he walk with a limp or have a funny little skip? Does she walk as though her hips don't belong to her body, or as though she's carrying a great weight in her stomach?
- Is one of her senses heightened? Does she have a particularly strong sense of smell? Does he have such keen hearing that he knows all the secrets in a house?
- How does your character dress? Does he hide himself in baggy clothes that smother his lithe frame? Does she favor makeup with glitter, in colors that make her eyelids scream? Is his clothing a statement to the world, or an extension of his body?
- How does your character experience himself in his body? In contrast, how do others see him? Does he view himself as gawky and skinny when the world sees a tall, handsome young man? Does she consider herself elegant, even though the people in her life actually see her as snobby and uptight? Look at contrasts between your character's experience of himself and how other characters perceive him; you'll discover an entire world of gray that lends itself to wonderful character development and conflict.

- What would your character like to change about herself? What does your character love most about herself?

The Body Electric: On Sensory Imagery

While we're on the subject of the body, remember that characters are more than their words and thoughts; they are also their bodies. As people, we don't experience much separation of the self and the body unless we are in shock, experiencing trauma, or suffering from post-traumatic stress disorder. Remember to keep your characters *embodied*—in other words, make sure to ground their emotions and experiences in sensory details. I talk about this throughout the book, because sensory cues are the most powerful way to draw readers directly into a character's experiences. Constantly think of your character's body—how she inhabits it, how she wields it, what she does and does not do with it. What permission does she give to other people to come in contact with her, and in what ways? What parts of herself does she withhold from contact? Think of literal and metaphoric imagery that illustrates these concepts.

Here is some literal imagery from *The Small Backs of Children*, as a character named "The Poet" awakens after a long flight, bleary and tired:

> She sees the world on its side, blurry and colored like waking is. She sees what must be the hairs of her own arm foresting up in front of her. She wets her lips with her tongue, which pulls her fully from sleep and activates the nerve-twine and vertebrae of her neck.

Now here is some imagery from the same book that is metaphoric and poetic:

> History and time open like a mouth, inside which pulses the small pang of an ordinary woman.

The body is at once personal and universal. We are all individuals, unique and different, but we all have bodies, and predominantly the same parts, at least to our genders. (Of course, if you or one of your characters is transgender, then you or they inhabit a much more complex continuum. This, by the way, can lend itself to some powerful writing.) The most vivid characters let us intimately into their bodily experience, reminding us that we are not so different. We bleed and bruise, chew and digest, kiss and make love, and in the realm of fiction, these bodily moments reveal many things about the characters experiencing them.

The chapters that follow invite you to reveal these embodied cues to the reader, transforming simple sentences into powerful, vivid, beating, unforgettable human lives.

ENGAGE YOUR CHARACTERS

It's wonderful to know your character's fears and flaws, strengths and longings, but stories rely on characters doing more than feeling and thinking; they must jump into action, make messes for themselves, and climb into conflict with other characters. So a strong character takes action. Sometimes she takes it fearfully, full of doubts, even fighting back panic. Other times, she leaps with confidence into all manner of actions. We'll talk more about this in chapter twelve, but this issue is important to keep in mind when you design your characters, too. Are you creating a character who has the chops to uncover secrets, fight opposing forces, learn and utilize new skills, and *do* something about her problems—or are you creating a character who elegantly muses upon her life in a quiet and reflective way? When I edit fiction manuscripts, I can't tell you how often I see wonderful characters in my clients' work who don't *do* enough.

WRITE IN SCENES

The most intricate nuances of POV will be lost upon a reader if you're not writing in scenes. Throughout this book we talk about using character cues to demonstrate emotion and invite readers close to your characters' experiences. A scene is the vehicle for turning passive experience into real-time, energizing movement.

Scenes depend on physical action and sensory imagery to create a simulacrum of real life. Scenes require settings—places the reader can see visually—to set the stage upon which plot drama can take place, and they mirror the larger plot structure with their own beginning, middle, and end. Point of view allows you to refine the proximity, or intimacy, between readers and the character, and shape how you demonstrate your characters' feelings, reactions, and consequences.

NOW YOU

CREATE A CHARACTER SCAFFOLDING

Build a character by answering the following questions:

- Do you want an intimate POV or a distant one? (Right now, deciding based on your best guess or a gut feeling is okay. After you read Part Two, you can come back and make a final decision.)
- What are some telling visual details about your character?
- What is your character haunted by? What is his backstory wound?
- What is your character's flaw?
- Which of your character's strengths is only a glimmer now but will become fully realized by the story's end?
- What is the story problem? What call to change or adventure will the character receive?

HYBRIDIZE YOUR CHARACTER

Create a hybrid character from several people you know. Write a paragraph in which your character prominently demonstrates several traits or features from these various sources in an interaction with another character. Don't just tell readers which traits the character is exhibiting—show them through action.

EMBODY YOUR CHARACTER

Describe your character not by how she looks but by other aspects of how she inhabits and uses her body: the way she walks, a clothing choice that says a lot about her, or how close she lets people get to her physically. Put your character in a scene where she is uncomfortable or uncertain, or must pretend to be someone she's not. Discomfort and vulnerability make for great tension. Shoot for writing a page, but see if you can go longer.

2

TELL ME A STORY
Narrative Voice and Authorial Intrusion

"Speech is the voice of the heart."

—ANNA QUINDLEN

Even when it is based on true events, fiction is a constructed, stylized version of reality. Thus, it's impossible to paint every event, action, and detail you dream up onto the slender canvas of your novel. Using only words, you must select your details carefully to create an outer landscape in the form of setting, which readers can picture in their minds, and a character with an inner landscape so vivid that readers feel they are sharing the same room and possibly even the same body. You are the puppeteer behind the scenes, deciding how much information to present to readers at any given time, and through which filter or "lens" (a character's point of view). You must limit information purposefully to omit boring bits that don't drive your story forward. At the same time, you have to maintain the reader's interest by doling out a little information at a time, like bits of cheese that tempt a mouse deeper into a maze.

Some stories are told by an omniscient narrator, like a supreme being who knows all and sees all, and who can deliver information to readers as necessary to further the story. However, even a godlike narrator doesn't give away the bank all at once. Think of the omniscient narrator as the Internet of your story. This narrator has access to any and all information about the characters, their feelings and history, and the story's plot points, and offers it only as needed.

Most readers want to open a book and sink into the story immediately. They don't want to be preoccupied with distracting questions about who is telling the story or how the narrator knows certain information. If readers begin to notice inconsistencies or ask questions such as "Is the character or the writer telling this story?" then you haven't quite mastered the art of narrative voice. In order to use it to best effect, you must first understand its structure and purpose.

THE PURPOSE OF NARRATIVE VOICE

Characters *demonstrate* their behavior in four ways: through actions, dialogue, thoughts, and feelings. Yet a great deal of information and detail in a story doesn't fall neatly within these categories. Setting descriptions, observations, philosophies, sensory imagery, and more fall in the cracks between action, dialogue, and thoughts. All of that in-between material constitutes your narrative voice.

Think of narrative voice as the stream in which the story flows, carrying along the key information a story needs to thrive. Or, if you prefer a more personified approach, think of the narrative voice as an impartial court reporter sharing with the reader (and often the character) that Harry Potter is a wizard, that Jane Eyre doesn't believe Mr.

Rochester could love her, or that *Gone Girl*'s "Amazing Amy" is not the sweet, content housewife she appears to be.

Narrative voice reports the thoughts, feelings, and opinions of your characters *indirectly*. It differs from internal monologue (thought) and dialogue in that it is an ongoing stream of observation and sensory information that tells readers a story without relying on the character to do so. However, narrative voice must feel organic to your character. Its tone and style should not be vastly different from your character's manner of thought and speech, unless your narrator really *is* a separate person from the protagonist, like Nick Carraway, who tells Gatsby's story in *The Great Gatsby*.

Here's an example of narrative voice in the novel *How to Tell Toledo from the Night Sky* by Lydia Netzer:

> Irene kept her face steady, her eyes open, pointed at the machine. If she worked until her face melted into the detector, if her brain fell down into the path of the accelerator, if it was penetrated by pions and if a small black hole was created in her skull, then at least she would have finished all the data for this set. She blinked her eyes to wake herself up, clicked the knob, and peered into the machine, like every time before.

We gather much information about Irene—what she thinks and sees—from this paragraph. However, she isn't reporting to us directly using "I" statements. Some of the details are simple ones that set the scene: "Irene kept her face steady, her eyes open ..." Contrast this with the same description in first person: "I steady my face and keep my eyes open."

When we read the line "If a small black hole was created in her skull, then at least she would have finished all the data for this set," we understand these are Irene's thoughts as she is performing this precarious, and potentially dangerous, scientific work. But these thoughts are not presented in italics (indicating active thought within the scene), nor is the tag "she thought" present anywhere in the excerpt. Calling attention to her thoughts would distract from the scene, whereas delivering them in the fluid form of narrative voice holds our attention. When characters' thoughts are extrapolated into their own lines, it calls attention to them and jars the reader from the flow of reading. In essence, the narrative voice attempts to offer as seamless a description of events and feelings as possible in a scene to keep the reader's attention. It is *of* the character's point of view but not *in* it.

Here's another example, from Liane Moriarty's novel *Big Little Lies*:

> His tone was light and humorous, as if he weren't really taking any of it seriously, although, knowing Perry, the lightness was probably a cover. He had a particular paranoia about bullying because of his own experiences as a child. He was like a secret service guy when it came to his boys, his eyes darting about suspiciously, monitoring the park or the playground for rough kids or savage dogs or pedophiles posing as grandfathers.

Here, the narrative voice belongs to a character named Celeste, who is observing her husband, Perry, and their sons at the school playground. Though she is providing information about Perry, we know she is not in the omniscient viewpoint. She gives us cues that these are *her* thoughts and opinions with words like "as if" and "knowing Perry." And, once again, her thoughts are not pulled out and separated from the flow of information. The author could have had Celeste think these things in a more distracting way, such as: *"Perry can be so paranoid,* she thought," but this would interrupt the flow of the story and prove distracting for the reader.

Narrative voice is how you deliver the most character information with the least disruption to story flow. Everything else is action, dialogue, or thoughts. In between, narrative voice flows like water over rocks.

NARRATIVE VOICE AND POINT OF VIEW

If narrative voice is the stream of your story, then point of view is like the swimmer stroking through it, offering sensation, feelings, and action directly. The narrative voice of your story will feel slightly different depending on which point of view you use, however. For example, when writing in first person, the narrative voice will merge with the character's thoughts. In other points of view, the narrative voice can be presented in the character's viewpoint or that of an omniscient, godlike storyteller. When considering how narrative voice and POV interact in your novel, first ask whether the POV is *internal* or *external* to your character.

As I've mentioned before, readers love to follow characters they feel close to—with whom they feel *intimate*. While that word might make you giggle, intimacy in fiction means that readers understand a character deeply and see her strengths, flaws, vulnerabilities, and maturity. Choosing an internal POV makes the character *self-aware* (in which she delivers personal observations, thoughts, and feelings internally), while an external POV makes that character *opaque* (in which information is delivered about the character externally). This POV choice will also affect the narrative voice and the degree of intimacy between reader and character.

Narrative Voice and Internal POVs

An internal POV makes readers feel as though they are right inside the mind and heart of the character, or that they *are* the character. Several points of view are considered internal: first person, second person, and third-person intimate. Notice in the examples that follow how close you feel to the character.

First Person

The first person is the most intimate point of view available. We are inside the character's mind and heart directly—no secondary or omniscient sources required. Here's an example of this POV from Krassi Zourkova's novel *Wildalone*:

> I recognized him intuitively—his voice, the way he said my name. Then I saw the silhouette. The white flower in his hand. But also something else: unmistakably different body, unfamiliar face. For one last instant, my brain refused to accept it. Then I was hit with the obvious truth:
> This had to be the guy from my concert. And it wasn't Rhys.
> Before I could react, he smiled and came up to me. The slow, cautious moves again, stopping just as his body was about to touch mine.

In this example, the narrative voice and the POV are one and the same. The character's thoughts, feelings, and observations are reported directly to the reader from within. The character's revelation—that the "guy from the concert" isn't Rhys but someone else entirely—is delivered in her point of view, and the reader assumes this is her thought, even though she never says, "I thought." Notice the intimacy, the way the *I* pronoun renders the line between reader and character null. Every detail, every feeling, seems to belong to you.

Second Person

It's rare to find an entire book written in the second person; it can be a strangely self-conscious manner of narration that is difficult to sustain for several hundred pages (though I will touch on several examples in later chapters). Instead it's often used when a character who is narrating in first person expresses a universal thought, truth, or experience, as in this excerpt from Myfanwy Collins's tragic YA novel *The Book of Laney*:

> To begin with tracking, you examine the track from three perspectives—lying, standing, and flying. Lying down is when you get all close and personal with your track, planting your nose as near it as possible. Standing allows you to take a look at the trail, not just the track. Flying is when you use what you know of the surrounding ecology to bring perspective to the track. Also

important is whatever it is that the animal has stepped in, like mud or snow.

Most of this novel is written in first person; however, the *you* pronoun is used in this passage as a way of thinking about the self universally. The character is considering that anyone who might be tracking could find themselves in this situation and would have to "examine the track from three perspectives," "get all close and personal with your track," and so on. In this case, *you* is a generalized pronoun that both refers to the character and to an imagined "someone" who might also undertake tracking.

Third-Person Intimate

This is one of the most versatile perspectives because it allows readers to be intimate with your character but also provides a smidge of distance. The following example comes from Jennifer McMahon's novel *The Winter People*:

> "Wake up, Martin." A soft whisper, a flutter against his cheek. "It's time."
>
> Martin opened his eyes, leaving the dream of a woman with long dark hair. She'd been telling him something. Something important, something he was not supposed to forget.
>
> He turned over in bed. He was alone. Sara's side of the bed cold. He sat up, listening carefully. Voices, soft giggles across the hall, from behind Gertie's bedroom door.
>
> Had Sara spent the whole night in with Gertie again?

Here, the reader feels and sees only what Martin does, but the effort of using his name or the pronoun *he* allows a bit of distance. We certainly don't feel as close to this character as we would if the passage were presented in first-person POV. The narrative voice and the point of view are a hair's breadth apart, creating a slight distance from the incredibly intense subject matter of the novel, which could be difficult to read in first person.

Writing the Intimate Character

Narrative Voice and External Omniscience

On the other end of the intimacy spectrum are the external viewpoints, in which readers observe a character from an omniscient or remote vantage point, looking in on the character from the outside. The most common external POV in fiction is omniscient (sometimes referred to as third-person objective, but I think this label is confusing for writers who are trying to distinguish third-person intimate from omniscient). This POV presents information to the reader that the character already knows about himself (physical descriptions of himself, personal traits, etc.) and is thus unlikely to report or even think about. Narrative voice is used to communicate information to readers that the character doesn't report directly.

Take these examples from Lauren Groff's literary novel *Fates and Furies*. Notice the first description is in omniscient. The description is external to Lotto; these are not things he would think himself:

> Lotto was a tiny adult, articulate, sunny. … Everyone worked to please, and Lotto, having no other models, pleased as well.

Then watch as Groff shifts between internal and external narration in the rest of the passage. (Keep in mind that the passage remains in the omniscient POV, even though the author slips into an internal perspective throughout):

> Lotto got off his bike when he saw his father on the old pump, apparently napping. Odd. Gawain never slept during the day. The boy stood still. A woodpecker clattered against a magnolia. An anole darted over his father's foot. Lotto dropped the bike and ran, and held Gawain's face and said his father's name so loudly that he looked up to see his mother running, this woman who never ran, a screaming white swiftness like a diving bird.

Several details in this paragraph are internal to Lotto: He sees "his father on the old pump, apparently napping," and notes details about a woodpecker and an anole that are nearby. These observations are delivered through Lotto's eyes. The narrative voice also reports that Lotto thinks that his father's napping is "odd." Though he doesn't actively think this in scene, it is clear that this observation is coming from within.

However, details such as "the boy stood still" are external—we are no longer inside Lotto. Throughout the passage, the narrative voice describes him as "the boy."

As you can probably guess by now, writers often confuse internal and external perspectives. Always ask yourself: *Am I inside my character looking out, or am I outside my character looking in?* If you've selected the third-person intimate POV, you are limited to the internal—it's not much different from first person, except that you're using the pronouns *he*, *she*, and *they* instead of *I*. Yet you might find yourself jumping back and forth between internal and external vantages—offering an emotion (internal) and then leaping to describe your character's physical appearance (external). Doing so puts you squarely in the omniscient POV. While there is nothing wrong with this viewpoint, you should be careful to choose it consciously to avoid confusing your readers with authorial intrusion.

AUTHORIAL INTRUSION

Literary styles and conventions change over the decades. In the nineteenth century, when writers such as Charles Dickens were popular, the narrator often intruded upon the story by speaking some aside, tangent, or counterpoint directly to readers. In fact, it was commonplace to use the phrase "dear reader" when offering these asides.

In contemporary literature, however, this device is used much less frequently because authorial intrusions distract from the story. Imagine if you were watching a movie and suddenly spotted the microphone boom or the director's chair in the midst of a scene in which two characters were having a powerful interaction. You'd be distracted and jarred from the story, and you would probably wonder why that error wasn't cut from the movie. Likewise, if the director strolled onto

Writing the Intimate Character

the set in the middle of a scene and tossed out an observation about how lovely the star looked in her costume, or how menacing the villain seemed, you'd likely be annoyed and wish for the director to disappear so the movie could continue unhindered. Authorial intrusion is the writer's version of a director's gaffe. It occurs in first-person or third-person limited POVs when the author makes an appearance within the world of your characters by offering a judgment or observation that isn't filtered directly through the narrative voice, internal monologue, or dialogue exchanges.

Intrusion in the Omniscient

The only POV that lends itself to narrative asides and intrusions is omniscient, since there is no single narrator but rather an all-knowing being who can draw from any information, anywhere, at any time (within reason). It takes immense care to wield the omniscient POV well, and we'll discuss it more in chapter nine.

Here's another great example of the omniscient POV from Lauren Groff's *Fates and Furies*:

> A unity, marriage, made of discrete parts. Lotto was loud and full of light; Mathilde quiet, watchful. Easy to believe that his was the better half, the one that set the tone. It's true that everything he'd lived so far had steadily built toward Mathilde. That if his life had not prepared him for the moment she walked in, there would have been no *them*.
>
> The drizzle thickened to drops. They hurried across the last stretch of beach.
>
> [Suspend them there, in the mind's eye: skinny, young, coming through dark toward warmth, flying over the cold sand and stone. We will return to them. For now, he's the one we can't look away from. He is the shining one.]

We get multiple details in this passage that don't come from the internal perspective of the characters. Lotto likely doesn't think of himself as "loud and full of light." And the final paragraph gets downright distant and poetic—a narrator is waxing lyrical here, creating a mood and using language to evoke feelings that don't come directly from inside Lotto or Mathilde. The omniscient voice is separated visually from the rest of the passage by brackets, which the author uses throughout the book to mark her intentional authorial intrusions.

To hold a reader's interest, you should create an immersive experience as quickly as possible, whereby the reader forgets she is reading and drops into the story so wholly that separation between self and story disappears. Authorial intrusion, even when done well, shoves readers out of that experience, which then leads to a greater likelihood that they will put down your story.

Authorial intrusion in first-person or third-person intimate is a downright no-no. In first person, the narrative voice is comprised solely of a character's thoughts, observations, and opinions—the author should not make any appearance at all. And as I mentioned earlier in the chapter, third-person intimate is quite similar to first person; the only difference is the pronouns used.

THOUGHTS VERSUS NARRATIVE VOICE

You'll notice that in the examples of narrative voice in this chapter, information is communicated about a character's opinions and philosophy, the sorts of things you might also put in the form of thoughts, or *internal monologue*. Following are some examples that illustrate the difference between thought and narrative voice, as well as advice on when to use one or the other.

First- and Second-Person Internal Monologue

There are several ways to alert the reader that your character is thinking. The two most common ways are to format the thoughts in italics or to add a tag such as "he thought" or "she mused" to the end of the thought. When you're writing in first person, the narrative voice and

Writing the Intimate Character

the character's thoughts are deeply intertwined, and most of the time you won't need to highlight or identify thoughts as separate from the narrative voice.

The following example comes from Warren Ellis's edgy mystery *Crooked Little Vein*. We are introduced to the protagonist, P.I. Michael McGill, in the opening pages of the novel, as a hard-up, smack-talking private detective trying to jump-start his career. In this passage he is alone in his office:

> It occurs to me now that if I hadn't seen the man in black on the far side of the street at that exact second, I would probably still be brushing my teeth with bleach.
>
> But I did. The absolutely stereotypical man in black, with the shades and the earpiece and the stone face.
>
> And another, down the street.
>
> I leaned over. A third was outside the door to my building.
>
> And they were all looking up at my window.
>
> "Well, you always knew this could happen," I told myself, because there was no one else around to give me a hard time.

All the information in this excerpt is filtered through the first-person narrative voice. There are no highlighted thoughts. His phrase "it occurs to me now" tells us that he is looking back on past events, but otherwise his thoughts are fully integrated with the narrative voice.

Even in the first-person point of view, there will come a time when a character has to think something he can't say, particularly when he is in a scene with other characters. In this example from *The Book of Laney*, although the character is narrating in first person, she still uses occasional italics to emphasize select thoughts.

> The moon shone through my window on the night of the memorial service. My mother always told me never to look at a full moon through a window. Bad luck, she said. My luck could not have gotten any worse and so I openly stared at the moon.
>
> *What did you see, Moon? Did you witness these crimes? Will you forgive me, Moon?*

Here, the character, Laney, is speaking to the moon in her mind after a tragic event, almost like a child, separating the thought from her narrative voice. Since she doesn't speak the words aloud, they get their own emphasis. Collins uses this sort of emphasis infrequently, because not much is needed. Emphasizing thoughts too much within first-person POV will jar the reader out of the story's flow.

In other instances in *The Book of Laney*, the author chooses to format the character's visions or memories in italics to distinguish them from the narrative voice:

> The pressure, now familiar and almost welcome to me, filled my head. My eyes were neither shut nor open, and I saw us walking across the lake in winter: *me, West, Alice. No, I didn't actually see us. I was there. I was as I was then and maybe I wasn't walking.*

Third-Person Intimate Thoughts

There are lots of ways to cue readers to a character's perspective in the third-person POV. Words like *recognized, noted, thought, considered,* and *reflected* all tell the reader that your character is thinking, that these thoughts belong to him.

In third-person *intimate*, thoughts can either be emphasized in italics or hinted at with certain cue words, as in this passage from Elizabeth Rosner's novel *Electric City*. The character, a mathematician named Steinmetz, has arrived at a mostly uninhabited cabin to do some work. He finds a giant mirror shattered on the floor:

> Foolish to have kept a mirror in a cabin, he chided himself.
> Instead of stooping in agitation toward the mess, wondering how to restore peace so he might work, Steinmetz felt the spark of an idea. Why not investigate this ordinary mystery? Find a way to harness nature's own extravagant power? In one pocket, his fingers curled around the shape of a book of matches; the skin on his forehead tingled and his jaw tightened around the still-unlit cigar. To start with, the damage left by this electrical visitation could be preserved with the faithful box camera he kept on

a bookshelf by the window. He could gather evidence of the path of discharge. Track it like some wild animal.

The first cue word in this excerpt is *chided*. To chide is to scold, and since he doesn't literally say to himself that it was foolish to have kept a mirror in the cabin, we can assume from *chided* that these are his thoughts. The phrase "felt the spark of an idea" lets us know that the sentences that follow are thoughts, considerations, and opinions coming from Steinmetz's perspective.

Omniscient Thoughts

In omniscient POV, because you have the stylistic freedom to move in and out of internal and external vantage points as needed without having to start a new scene or introduce a new character, it's important to give the reader more specific cues when you shift from narrative voice to thoughts.

Ingrid Hill's novel *Ursula, Under* traces the history of the ancestors of a little girl named Ursula, who falls down a mine shaft at the beginning of the novel. The story introduces multiple characters, and thus multiple perspectives. The author writes in the omniscient viewpoint to allow herself the latitude to travel from mind to mind over a long span of time.

In this scene, Ursula Wong, out walking with her parents, has just fallen into an abandoned mine shaft that none of them knew was there. The narrative voice takes liberties by entering the minds of both her parents, Annie and Justin, at the same time, something a limited perspective would not allow.

> Annie raises herself on her cane and stumbles toward him. They stand transfixed, staring down. The opening into which Ursula has fallen is amazingly small, and they can see nothing but darkness. They certainly cannot see Ursula herself.
>
> Neither of them wants to call out to her, unconsciously afraid their voices will echo back at them from too deep an emptiness.

Both of them think: *What is this? How deep?* and *Dear God, no.*
Both of them think: *A mine shaft?* Neither says the word.

In the next paragraph, the POV shifts temporarily to Annie:

> Annie had tried to imagine the shaft into which her grandfather
> descended one August day three-quarters of a century ago and
> from which he did not come out alive: fifteen hundred feet deep.
> No one could survive such a fall ... but is this such a shaft? Annie
> is telling herself, no, it must be something else.

Later in the same scene, the narrative voice moves to Justin's POV:

> Justin runs to the truck, his work boots seeming to shake the
> ground. The cell phone lies on the front seat, tiny and useless
> amid a scattering of animal crackers. In crisis the mind focuses
> on minutiae: he thinks, *Now is that cookie a rhinoceros or a hippo-*
> *potamus?* He picks up the phone. No signal. *Of course, no signal:*
> *there are no towers out here in the wilderness.*

No matter which character's head the author has chosen to occupy,
it's always clear who is thinking based on the use of cue words, such
as *imagine*, or the italicized formatting. When the POV shifts from
Annie to Justin, the author uses the character's name and a new paragraph to signal the switch.

NOW YOU

GET INTIMATE

If you haven't already, decide on the POV for your character. Choose
an existing scene, or write a new one in which your character feels a
strong emotion that requires sensory imagery (loathing, passion, regret). Now increase the intimacy. If you're writing in third person, for
instance, rewrite a page in first person. If you're already in first person

but you're using past-tense verbs, switch to present tense. If you're in omniscient, choose any of the intimate POVs.

BE THOUGHTFUL

Select an existing paragraph, or write a fresh one, in which you use third-person narrative voice to show your character learning a difficult piece of information in a scene where she doesn't have the ability or permission to speak her feelings aloud.

First, try integrating the thoughts into the narrative voice. Next, use italics to separate the thoughts. Notice the difference, and decide which method feels more organic to your scene or story.

TELL IT LIKE IT IS
Exposition and Point of View

*"The novelist says in words
what cannot be said in words."*

—URSULA K. LE GUIN

When characters aren't acting, speaking, or thinking, what remains is exposition, the in-between material. This chapter takes a closer look at the different kinds of exposition that fall between action and dialogue, and examines how to handle them well in each point of view.

If you use too much exposition, your story may feel like a lecture, and you run the risk of neglecting character development and slowing the pace. If you don't use enough exposition, though, you could end up with "talking-head syndrome," in which characters are all talk and no action or contemplation. Neglecting exposition can also make for a difficult-to-visualize setting that leaves readers grasping to figure out where your characters are. We'll explore how to wield key types of exposition in each point of view so that you don't fall into authorial intrusion. You'll also learn how to tell if you're inadvertently using omniscient.

SETTING EXPOSITION

As writers, we are limited by our medium. We do not have vivid colors of paint or celluloid imagery at our disposal—we have only small alphabetic symbols with which we must render entire worlds, fully realized people, and their ensuing actions. So while setting—the visual world of the story and its rich details—is an important expository element, you must render it carefully so as not to overwhelm or underwhelm the reader.

The key to developing a strong setting while staying integrated in your point of view is to do so through character interaction and observation. Try to steer clear of flat descriptions of the setting, which are often told omnisciently. We don't need a history of the entire South in order to set the scene in a particular homestead (though, of course, period details will need to be filtered through characters' observations, too). Instead, show us your character engaged with her setting: how she walks through it, what she observes and notices about it, how she feels about it. Doing so allows you to filter every detail through your character's experience. Keep in mind, too, that setting is a powerful opportunity to build tension, communicate information, create metaphors and foreshadowing, and have your character interact with the setting—kick over a chair, smooth a rumpled bed, wash a pile of long-unwashed dishes—if he is the only one in the scene.

Setting in First-Person Exposition

The science fiction novel *Ready Player One* by Ernest Cline is set in a dystopian future in which most citizens live, work, and play in a computer-simulated virtual reality called OASIS. To introduce us to the futuristic setting, Cline doesn't clutter the opening with a bunch of descriptions right off the bat, but he does use exposition to show the actual (nonvirtual) world of his protagonist, Wade. In the following passage, everything is revealed through Wade's point of view; he's either interacting with his setting, observing it, or expressing an opinion about it in the narrative voice:

> I was jolted awake by the sound of gunfire in one of the neighboring stacks. The shots were followed by a few minutes of muffled shouting and screaming, then silence.
>
> Gunfire wasn't uncommon in the stacks, but it still shook me up. I knew I probably wouldn't be able to fall back asleep, so I decided to kill the remaining hours until dawn by brushing up on a few coin-op classics. Galaga, Defender, Asteroids. ...
>
> I was curled up in an old sleeping bag in the corner of the trailer's tiny laundry room, wedged in the gap between the wall and the dryer. I wasn't welcome in my aunt's room across the hall, which was fine by me. I preferred to crash in the laundry room, anyway. It was warm, it afforded me a limited amount of privacy, and the wireless reception wasn't too bad. ...

The setting is described only as it relates to Wade's immediate experiences, but it still provides a potentially larger context—after all, how many people live in a world where gunfire is a common occurrence? There's nothing in this scene that isn't perceived by one of Wade's five senses, and yet it's not all delivered in potent sensory imagery—it's expository, straightforward description. It gets the job done quickly. However, you won't always be able to rely on exposition—eventually, to draw us into a character's experiences, you'll need to rely on strong sensory imagery.

Setting in Third-Person Intimate Exposition

In the following scene from Ellen Meister's humorous literary novel *Farewell, Dorothy Parker*, well-known movie critic Violet Epps, whose muse is the sharp-tongued writer Dorothy Parker, is having lunch at Parker's New York City haunt, the Algonquin Hotel, with her classless boyfriend. The setting is so famous, it's almost a character itself, and it would be easy to write a long, detailed passage describing its every nuance. But doing so would put readers to sleep. Instead, Meister gives us just enough detail to visualize the hotel as Violet experiences and moves through it. Then the author uses her prodigious skill to slide into exposition, as Violet imagines the room alive with the fascinating characters who once dined at the hotel:

> A few heads turned as they were led to the Round Table Room, which was really just a section in the back of the open lobby. As they made their way past people relaxing in the overstuffed chairs and sofas of the hotel's famous lounge, Violet heard someone quoting from one of her crankier reviews: *The best thing I can say about* By the Longhairs *is that people who have been given two months to live might be dead before it comes out on DVD. ...*
>
> Violet closed her eyes and tried to summon strength from her surroundings. She imagined the room abuzz with chatter as the members of the Algonquin Round Table ate and drank and traded quips. They were a group of writers and actors who met here for lunch every day for ten years, and their bon mots were printed in newspapers, laughed at over morning coffee, repeated in offices, and celebrated in speakeasies. But the most quoted of them all was Dorothy Parker.

Even though Meister chose third-person POV, all of the information is still being filtered through Violet's perspective. Once again, only that which Violet knows and sees is presented to the reader. And while we don't receive hundreds of specific details about the setting, we get enough to get a sense of the place and Violet's feelings about it.

Setting in Omniscient Exposition

In Lydia Netzer's literary novel *How to Tell Toledo from the Night Sky*, the author draws heavily on exposition in the omniscient point of view to dip in and out of time and her characters' perspectives, and to deliver information to the reader that the characters may not be able to know in a given scene:

At the time her mother fell down the stairs to her death in Toledo, Irene was far away in Pittsburgh, working in a lab. As her mother bounced down a flight of stairs in a bright city on the sparkling shore of Lake Erie, Irene sat in a dark room, in the basement of an ugly building, in a drab university, in an abandoned steel town. Irene's mother was named Bernice. They had not spoken to each other in years.

Irene pulled her lab coat around her and stared intently into a small glass window on a large metal apparatus. She wasn't thinking about her mother at all. In fact, all she was thinking about was her work. As her mother landed at the bottom of the stairs, arms and legs cracking, Irene concentrated only on recording the data from her machine.

In this opening paragraph, which manages to be both disturbing and slightly comical, Netzer could easily have chosen to deliver the two separate scenes—Irene working in her lab, and her mother falling to her death—in each character's perspective. However, the use of the omniscient POV allows the author to do several things. First, she can describe what might be a boring setting—Irene's lab—in a way that holds our attention, juxtaposed as it is with Bernice's fall; who can look away from a woman falling to her death? Second, she can capture Irene's mother's death in a physical way, through setting details, which she couldn't do as effectively inside Bernice's perspective, as a fall of that kind would happen too quickly for Bernice to offer the action words. Yet it's important to remember that the omniscient voice is not the author herself intruding into the story but rather a story-teller who belongs to the story itself—the narrative voice.

VISUAL IMAGERY EXPOSITION

The goal of every story is to allow the reader access to the experiences of your characters so that he connects and feels as though he is inside them. To accomplish this feat, you must trigger in the reader all of the senses that make real life so, well, real. Sensory imagery is the method by which you bring two-dimensional words on a page to three-dimensional life. When you can elicit smell, touch, taste, sight, sound, and emotions with your words, you're much more likely to hook your readers from the beginning. In later chapters we'll discuss character emotions in much more depth, but for the purposes of this chapter, we will explore how visual imagery allows readers to "see" your character's physical world and get a visual snapshot of other characters as well.

When your characters observe and interact with the world around them, you must be sure to draw from your copious tool belt of expository imagery to demonstrate what a beautiful sunny day looks like; or how a torrential downpour feels and smells; or the way an ancient barn sits, forlorn and slumping like an old dog; or how a mountaintop villa looms with the prescient intensity of a bird of prey.

Before we look at how to demonstrate such imagery in each point of view, it's important to point out that the exposition in your novel is never *just* describing the visual world, the setting, the weather, and other people. You are describing these things either through the eyes of a character—which means in the viewpoint of that particular character, with all of her unique history and feelings—or through the stylized omniscient voice of a narrator crafted specifically to deliver your story. In a novel, exposition should never be just *you* intruding on the story. This is why sensory exposition can sometimes be the most difficult to write—you must still manage to embody your characters as you describe something as basic as breakfast, or as simple as a skirt.

Visual Imagery in First-Person Exposition

In first person, readers see the world directly, as though they are interacting with it. In this passage from Donna Tartt's *The Goldfinch*, young Theo, the protagonist, is at a New York museum with his mother. While his mother obsesses over a painting she adores—the titular goldfinch—Theo watches a young girl with her grandfather. Notice how the exposition that describes her is refracted through Theo's eyes:

> Beautiful skin: milky white, arms like carved marble. Definitely
> she looked athletic, though too pale to be a tennis player; maybe

> she was a ballerina or a gymnast or even a high diver, practicing late in shadowy indoor pools, echoes and refractions, dark tile. Plunging with arched chest and pointed toes to the bottom of the pool, a silent *pow*, shiny black swimsuit, bubbles foaming and streaming off her small, tense frame.

We can surmise that the person who notices all of these details is a sensitive, keenly observant, even poetic person, as evidenced by how he describes the girl's "arms like carved marble" and the precise specificity of the details he conjures when looking at her. His exposition reveals a person who notices nuance and detail, traits which are also present in his adult character. It also suggests loneliness—he is an only child who doesn't see his father, who has grown up in the bustle of New York. So the exposition describes the girl, but it *reveals* Theo's character.

Visual Imagery in Third-Person Intimate Exposition

Lauren Groff's novel *Arcadia* roves through the third-person intimate POVs of several different characters, but it is really the story of Bit, a boy born on a secluded commune formed by his hippie parents and their friends in upstate New York and cut off from the rest of the world. His is a life in which boundaries often blur, and no one ever explains to him why his mother becomes so sad that she can't get out of bed, or why she is eventually taken away for some time.

In this scene, Bit gets lost in the woods outside their commune after dark. Terrified and unsure what to do, he observes the following:

> From the corner of his eye, he sees a white movement. He watches it obliquely for ten breaths, then turns his head to look. He expects to see one of the stones crawling off into the darkness, but it is not a stone.
>
> An animal stands there, pointy and white and tall, fringed. It is graceful as a white deer, but it is not a deer.

The beast fixes Bit with its yellow eye and sniffs. At its side, the shadows thicken. The texture flows vertical and becomes fabric. Bit holds himself tiny and still, and looks up the dress to find a face. A woman stares at him, a very old woman. It is the witch, the one he has dreamed of. But she is not ugly: her hair is a soft white with a black streak, and she has roses in her cheeks.

Most of the visual exposition, in third-person intimate, is straightforward, described as literally as a child would see it: the animal is "pointy and white and tall"; the "shadows thicken"; her hair is "a soft white." But this passage—most likely a hallucination—is also fraught with thematic information. For what does he see at his most terrified but an old *woman*? She may be the "witch" of his dreams, but she turns out to be kind and not ugly. As a reader, it's hard not to see her as the representation of the wisdom and guidance Bit so desperately needs but does not receive from the adults in his life.

Visual Imagery in Omniscient Exposition

We've already looked once at Ingrid Hill's epic historical novel *Ursula, Under,* which uses omniscient POV to tell the stories of several ancestors of a little girl who is stuck in an abandoned mineshaft. In the following passage, a French Jesuit priest named René Josserand is recounting his day. However, the exposition in this scene isn't presented intimately in third person but is rendered in the more remote omniscient viewpoint, which provides just enough visuals to "see" the scene:

There is little about the day to day of this journey that smacks of glamour. There are wretched rapids to the rivers that overturn the boats dozens of times, causing a frightening concussion to Josserand with an aftermath of recurring headaches, and a ripped thigh muscle and broken elbow to Le Boîte. There are raggedy shorelines to the lakes that, because of the danger of the beautiful but treacherous open water, necessitate closely hugging the ins and outs of the wild coast and thus doubling the distance.

There are swarms of fat bloodsucking insects and leeches and snakes whose benignity or danger is uncertain.

Notice that the exposition in the omniscient POV shows the scenery but doesn't go into any specific detail because it isn't filtered through Josserand's senses. Omniscient also can tell us information about multiple characters because it doesn't require the intimate viewpoint of a single character's experience. Readers get the gist, but they will eventually crave specificity and more robust sensory and visual images so they can truly share in the characters' experiences. However, to move the story along, which is what exposition does best, this passage serves its function perfectly.

PERSONAL AND THEMATIC PHILOSOPHY EXPOSITION

Aside from dialogue, actions, and thoughts, one of the most powerful ways to develop characters is to allow their opinions and beliefs to slip through the cracks of the narrative voice. This is what I call *personal philosophy*. People, real and fictional, are informed by their histories, their beliefs, and their opinions. They make statements or observations in the vein of this personal philosophy in and around the action of scenes. While a large amount of personal philosophy is often a hallmark of literary fiction, it is showing up more frequently in genre fiction, too, as a way to show the reader what kind of person your character is.

This is also a way of expressing and handling the themes of your novels, revealing the deeper issues that underscore both character and plot.

Philosophical musings have a slower pace, however, so you shouldn't toss one into the middle of an intense action scene, or in a place in the story where you are trying to increase the tension. These expository musings provide pause, reflection, and insight during quieter points in the story.

When it isn't delivered in dialogue or thoughts, a character's philosophy must come through in the exposition of narrative voice, directly and plainly.

Philosophy in First-Person Exposition

The fantasy novel *Fool's Errand* by Robin Hobb is the first in The Tawny Man trilogy. The protagonist, FitzChivalry Farseer, is possessed of the unique ability to merge with the minds of others and see visions of other places—a talent known as "Skilling." Fitz has lived in self-imposed exile for fifteen years and is presumed dead, having survived an assassin's attack by temporarily projecting his mind into the body of his pet wolf. In the following passage, he is visited by his old mentor-teacher, Chade, who has found him after all these years. Notice how exposition is used to show Fitz's philosophy on his life:

> He came one late, wet spring, and brought the wide world back to my doorstep. I was thirty-five that year. When I was twenty, I would have considered a man of my current age to be teetering on the verge of dotage. These days, it seemed neither young nor old to me, but a suspension between the two. I no longer had the excuse of callow youth, and I could not yet claim the eccentricities of age. In many ways, I was no longer sure what I thought of myself. Sometimes it seemed that my life was slowly disappearing behind me, fading like footprints in the rain, until perhaps I had always been the quiet man living an unremarkable life in a cottage between the forest and the sea.

There is no dialogue or action in the scene, only philosophical musing, in which Fitz ponders the meaning of age, of what he believed about it once, and of what he believes about it now. It contains metaphoric language: "brought the wide world back to my doorstep" and "fading like footprints in the rain." It is a musing on the passage of time, and of the nature of aging. These passages shouldn't go on for too long, because too much reflection eventually slows the story's pace. However, well-placed snippets of personal philosophy add texture and nuance to your character.

Philosophy in Third-Person Intimate Exposition

Let's look at a third-person intimate passage from Liane Moriarty's *Big Little Lies*, in which Celeste's musings about her husband, Perry, serve to show her philosophy, which helps her justify a very bad situation:

> Perry's rage was an illness. A mental illness. She saw the way it took hold of him, how he tried his best to resist. When he was in the throes of it, his eyes became red and glassy, as if he were drugged. The things he said didn't even make sense. It wasn't him. The rage wasn't him. Would she leave him if he got a brain tumor and the tumor affected his personality? Of course she wouldn't.
>
> This was just a glitch in an otherwise perfect relationship. Every relationship had its glitches. Its ups, its downs. It was like motherhood. Every morning the boys climbed into bed with her for a cuddle, and at first it was heavenly, and then, after about ten minutes or so, they started fighting, and it was terrible. Her boys were gorgeous little darlings. Her boys were feral little animals.

The reader knows that Celeste is attempting to explain to herself what can't logically be explained. These snippets of philosophy reveal her complex set of beliefs, which help keep her in this terrible situation. She even goes so far as to compare her abusive husband to naturally argumentative children, which is a stretch for even the most understanding personality. This scene is sad and powerful, but, more important, it helps us understand Celeste's motivations and reasons for putting up with the abuse—because she believes it isn't Perry's fault.

Without these glimpses into philosophy, the reader can't completely understand a character's motivation. Philosophy helps explain important details to the reader. The key is to offer it up sparingly so you don't hinder the story's pace or give away too much too soon.

Philosophy in Omniscient Exposition

Ann Patchett's novel *Bel Canto* is written in the omniscient viewpoint. The author weaves information from the POVs of multiple characters and different moments in time—flashing back, flashing forward—and offers philosophical musings that come not from a particular character but from an omniscient narrator. This is a novel about the art of music, how it touches us all differently, and how different people with different backgrounds and intentions can connect through music.

The following scene takes place during a lavish party thrown in honor of the Japanese businessman Mr. Hosokawa, at the home of the vice president of an unnamed South American country. The entertainment features a world-famous, much beloved opera soprano, Roxane Coss. The omniscient narrator delivers a bit of philosophical musing after Hosokawa kisses Coss at the end of her performance. Notice that the questions and musings in this passage aren't attached to a character's viewpoint—it is almost as though we, the readers, are the ones asking these questions:

> Would he have kissed her like that had the room been lit? Was his mind so full of her that in the very instant of darkness he reached for her, did he think so quickly? Or was it that they wanted her too, all of the men and the women in the room, and so they imagined it collectively? They were so taken by the beauty of her voice that they wanted to cover her mouth with their mouth, drink in. Maybe music could be transferred, devoured, owned. What would it mean to kiss the lips that had held such a sound?

The sentence "Maybe music could be transferred, devoured, owned" is especially philosophical and thematic, delivered without need of a character viewpoint. Omniscient POV allows more room to dally in these kinds of musings, so long as they don't stop or slow the action too much.

Sometimes in the omniscient POV, however, the musing will shift or "zoom" from the all-knowing narrator into the more intimate scope of one particular character. In the following passage from Donna Tartt's novel *The Little Friend*, Allison is one of two sisters whose brother, Robin, died years ago, mysteriously, leaving the family wrecked and traumatized. Allison was only four at the time of her older brother's death and does not appear to remember it. Yet the dreamy way she experiences the world could be likened to the aftermath of a traumatic event or even suggest suppressed memories.

Here, Tartt moves from a distant external viewpoint, which is used to describe what Allison remembers of the days after Robin died, to the intimate internal viewpoint of Allison's philosophical musing:

> How could you ever be perfectly sure when you were dreaming and when you were awake? In dreams you thought you were awake, though you weren't. And though it seemed to Allison that she was currently awake, sitting barefoot on her front porch with a coffee-stained library book on the steps beside her, that didn't mean she wasn't upstairs in bed, dreaming it all: porch, gardenias, everything.

Remember that exposition is everything else that flows between the most important aspects of character development: action, dialogue, and thought. The more consciously you learn to write exposition, the less likely that any sentence will feel superfluous or careless. Every sentence will be filtered through the eyes and personality of your characters, resulting in rich, immersive fiction.

NOW YOU

VOICE IN EXPOSITION

Experiment with crafting exposition that sounds like your character rather than yourself, regardless of the POV you choose. Either select an existing passage or write a fresh paragraph for each of the following expository aspects:

- **SETTING IMAGERY:** Pick a specific place and describe it through exposition as your character would describe it, filtering it through her eyes.
- **CHARACTER DESCRIPTION:** Imagine your character has to write a short biography about himself for an alumni magazine,

a local paper, or an organization he belongs to. How would it sound if he described himself?

- **PERSONAL PHILOSOPHY:** Your character is about to engage in a debate, a fight, or a confrontation with someone who sees the world very differently. Here, your character is coaching herself through her own beliefs and values, thinking about the ways she sees the world or a story problem differently from this antagonist.

Remember to let your words reflect the values and history of your character, as well as communicate basic information.

4

DO YOU FEEL ME?
Surface and Subset Character Emotions

"The best and most beautiful things in the world cannot be seen or even touched. They must be felt with the heart."

—HELEN KELLER

If point of view is the lens through which you demonstrate your character's experiences to readers, then emotions are the tools you utilize to provide the colors and shapes for every scene and to add depth and meaning to your character's inner life.

Why does emotion matter? Because what characters feel is the pulsing life force that flows through every sentence in your story. Events without emotion are just flatly narrated facts, a journalist's account that does little to trigger any emotional response or caring in readers. Characters without an emotional journey, who do not change and transform throughout the course of the novel, won't earn a reader's sympathy and concern. When you allow readers to understand, feel, and participate in your characters' feelings through the clear use of emotion in point of view, you create deep reader investment in your story. Demonstrating emotions is also the best way to communicate the impact of plot events without relying on tension-killing narrative summary.

THE WHEEL OF EMOTION: SURFACE AND SUBSET FEELINGS

In every scene, characters will experience and demonstrate two levels of emotion: *surface feelings* and *subset feelings*. Surface feelings are like the primary colors in a color wheel: They are the most essential, familiar, basic feelings a character can have, from which all other combinations of emotion will flow. The most basic surface feelings are:

- happiness
- sadness
- anger
- fear

In every scene, your character should display a basic surface feeling. To determine what it is, start by asking, "Is my character happy, sad, angry, or afraid?"

Once you figure out the surface feeling for a scene, you will need to go deeper to discover what other feelings are boiling below the surface. As literary agent and author Donald Maass writes in his book *The Fire in Fiction*, tension is present in a scene primarily when characters have conflicting emotions, when hurt wars with love, or when anger rubs up against desire. We'll look at many examples of how these conflicting emotions play out in action in chapters seven through ten.

You can excavate entire layers of feelings beneath the surface feeling. These layers are known as subset feelings. Let's break down each surface feeling into potential subset feelings and look at examples of sensory imagery or image-based analogies you might use to convey these feelings in an embodied way. Remember, these examples are just a few cues of my own invention, but there are hundreds of ways to convey these emotions uniquely with your characters.

Happiness

- Joy

    - **SENSORY CUE:** "He felt a tingling in the limbs, the rising or swelling of buoyancy, as if he was floating along a river."
    - **IMAGE CUE:** "Her chest filled with effervescence, like bubbles in a glass of champagne."

- Cheer

    - **SENSORY CUE:** "Warmth moved through him like a swig of hot tea."
    - **IMAGE CUE:** "He was suddenly unburdened, as though shrugging out of a heavy wool coat."

- Relief

    - **SENSORY CUE:** "She experienced a sudden lightness of the limbs—she might fly if she jumped."
    - **IMAGE CUE:** "He was struck by a gust of freedom as he tumbled to the ground. He'd felt it only once before, while winning a vigorous game of tug-of-war."

- Ecstasy

    - **SENSORY CUE:** "Her entire body was electric, as though her nerves were tiny circuits turned on all at once."
    - **IMAGE CUE:** "Being with him was like stepping into the perfect bath, its warmth all-encompassing, never to grow cold."

Sadness

- Grief

  - **SENSORY CUE:** "Weighted and dark, breath huddled in her lungs like heavy stones."
  - **IMAGE CUE:** "Grief stalked him like a mother wolf that has lost a cub, howling and insistent."

- Uncertainty

  - **SENSORY CUE:** "His fingers twitched as if they would choose for him, but his arm stiffened."
  - **IMAGE CUE:** "She balanced before him like a squirrel that wanted to eat the nuts in his outstretched hand, stuck on the edge of a choice."

- Defeat

  - **SENSORY CUE:** "For a moment, everything was numb: no air in his lungs, no electric currents of touch across nerve endings, just the utter absence of any feeling."
  - **IMAGE CUE:** "Her body folded like a building in collapse, detonated by her loss."

- Regret

  - **SENSORY CUE:** "Her heart didn't beat so much as kick at her rib cage in time with a litany of things she should have said instead."
  - **IMAGE CUE:** "Walking away felt like tossing a match on a home full of valuables."

In this second set of subset feelings, I offer shorthand bodily manifestations (things people do with their bodies) and common words or phrases that cue you to how these actions might manifest in your characters. This also shows you just how nuanced these levels of feeling are. The more you explore them, the more specific you can get:

Anger

- Hurt

  - **BODILY MANIFESTATIONS:** a drooping posture, closing or folding arms, turning away, covering one's face with hands, crying
  - **FEELING WORDS:** punched, gutted, heavy, bruised, tortured, kicked, dark, flattened, wrecked, ruined

- Resentfulness

  - **BODILY MANIFESTATIONS:** sneering or frowning, shaking one's head, glaring at the object of resentment, refusing to talk to someone, turning away sharply, using sarcasm in dialogue
  - **FEELING WORDS:** disgusted, taken for a ride, sour grapes, wishing for a do-over

- Frustration

  - **BODILY MANIFESTATIONS:** stomping, kicking or punching a wall or the ground, grinding one's teeth, shouting or moaning aloud, sighing or exhaling heavily, theatrically throwing things
  - **FEELING WORDS:** stuck, caught, defeated, aggravated, giving up, throwing in the towel

- Outrage

  - **BODILY MANIFESTATIONS:** screaming, freezing in place, yelling aloud or attacking another person, waving or shaking an object, stabbing a finger in the air, shaking a fist at someone
  - **FEELING WORDS:** horrified, appalled, galled, shocked, devastated, traumatized, uncomprehending, caught unawares

Fear

- Terror

  - **BODILY MANIFESTATIONS:** becoming paralyzed, freezing in place, whimpering, hunkering down, hiding, losing one's abil-

ity to speak, crying, peeing one's pants, blacking out, hyperventilating
- **FEELING WORDS:** scared, horrified, frozen, shocked, aghast, hypnotized, bewildered, trapped, suffocated, wrecked

- Worry

  - **BODILY MANIFESTATIONS:** grimacing, wringing one's hands, frowning, sighing, looking around, hugging oneself
  - **FEELING WORDS:** concerned, alarmed, afraid, wondering, befuddled

- Anxiety

  - **BODILY MANIFESTATIONS:** nervously twitching, shaking one's head repeatedly, breathing quickly, pacing, repeating words or phrases, running around in pursuit of an answer, speaking quickly
  - **FEELING WORDS:** disquieted, nervous, uncertain, troubled, wondering, feeling unresolved, awaiting an answer, distrusting

- Anguish

  - **BODILY MANIFESTATIONS:** collapsing in place, becoming immobile, sobbing, pleading and crying aloud, shouting, grasping after another person, neglecting oneself, refusing help
  - **FEELING WORDS:** despair, grief stricken, all is lost, devastated, crushed, done for

For most of us, the surface feeling in any given scene we write is already apparent; at least we have a pretty good idea of what it is. For example, if your scene involves a confrontation between your protagonist, who is an angry, jilted woman, and her two-timing lover, the surface feeling is likely anger. But what you might not find out until you've written the scene is that your protagonist feels other things, too, such as desire, frustration, hurt, and embarrassment.

In my book *Make a Scene*, I refresh the common writing adage "Show, don't tell" with "Demonstrate, don't narrate." In other words, let your characters act, speak, and reveal their feelings rather than resorting to either the narrative voice or authorial intrusion (see chapter two). You can communicate any and all emotional experiences through *character cues*.

ESSENTIAL CHARACTER CUES

In the realm of literature, simply having a character say or think what he's feeling, or using the narrative voice to tell the reader directly, is not nearly as effective as dramatizing the emotion. Consider these two examples, which convey the same emotional message—fear—but are markedly different. Which is more engaging?

> The man's face in the window scared her horribly.

> At the sight of the man's face in the window she tripped backwards over the chair and shrieked.

Similarly, you have a range of other methods at your disposal to show what a character is feeling or observing without having to explain directly. I refer to these methods as *character cues*. These cues provide information to readers about the character without having to explain flatly or describe something using exposition.

Depending on the point of view you've chosen, the cues to demonstrate character emotion will vary; we'll explore these differences in Part Two. For now, here are the basic cues you can use to demonstrate character emotion and experience.

Physical-Action Cues

As I demonstrated already, you can use body language and physical actions to show a character's emotion. Now let's look at some examples in contemporary fiction. In the following scene from Neil Gaiman's science fiction novel *Anansi Boys*, a character wakes in a state of terror on a plane. His physical actions communicate his desire to get the hell out of there:

He stood up and tried to get out to the aisle, tripping over people as he went past, then, when he was almost at the gangway, straightening up and banging the overhead locker with his forehead, which knocked open the locker door and tumbled someone's hand luggage down onto his head.

Sensory Cues

Hands down, one of the most important cues you will use in your fiction to convey emotion is sensory imagery: the character's perceptions of the world, as well as his feelings, filtered through the senses. This sensory imagery includes the touch, smell, sound, look, and taste of a character's experiences. You might write, "The salt of his sweat burned on her tongue," to convey desire, sensuality, or lust. Or if a character is keeping a terrible grief at bay, he might feel "dense and damp with tears that could not fall." Sensory imagery pulls readers inside your character's body, sets a tone or a mood, and conveys a potential feeling.

Here's an example from the novel *The Bees* by Laline Paull, in which she gives human characteristics to bees and dramatizes the life of one bee. In the first scene, the bee hatches from her honeycomb. Notice how you feel the character's definite sense of panic from the sensory imagery alone:

> The cell squeezed her and the air was hot and fetid. All the joints of her body burned from her frantic twisting against the walls, her head was pressed into her chest and her legs shot with cramp, but her struggles had worked—one wall felt weaker.

Dialogue Cues

It's most effective to allow your characters' words to speak their emotions and experiences, not necessarily by having them make direct emotional statements ("I'm so happy right now" or "This really freaks me out") but by having their dialogue *reflect* a specific emotion:

> "I can't believe I fell for your crap." He shook his head so hard, his hair fell into his eyes.

The words could convey frustration, remorse, or regret. This, cou- pled with the body language—the physical action cue—of shaking his head so hard it moves his bangs, reveals that he's more than just a little upset. And none of that information was flatly or directly told to the reader (i.e., "He was really frustrated.").

Here's an example from Jennifer Egan's Pulitzer Prize–winning novel, *A Visit from the Goon Squad.* In this scene Sasha has stolen a woman's wallet, but she hasn't told Alex this yet:

> Sasha felt the waiters eyeing her as she sidled back to the table holding her handbag with its secret weight. She sat down and took a sip of her Melon Madness Martini and cocked her head at Alex. She smiled her yes/no smile. "Hello," she said.
>
> The yes/no smile was amazingly effective.
>
> "You're happy," Alex said.
>
> "I'm always happy," Sasha said. "Sometimes I just forget."

In this scene, the direct exclamation of Sasha's feelings ("I'm always happy") is not so straightforward. It feels like she's being ironic, or making fun of Alex, or possibly attempting some wishful thinking; if she says it aloud, perhaps she can make it true. There's a lot of subtext to this simple exchange, which reminds us that sometimes characters convey as much by what they don't say as by what they do.

Other Character's Reactions

Other characters will react to your protagonist's situation, thus high- lighting his emotion or experience. If you want to show that a char- acter has said something hurtful, let the other character in the scene react in a hurt way, as in this example:

> Mary's eyes widened to discs, and she stepped away from me. "I can't believe you think that."

This next example comes from Cassandra Dunn's contemporary nov- el *The Art of Adapting.* In this example Lana's husband, Graham, left her seven months before, and she still hasn't adjusted to becoming a single mom on a solo income. She's not at all interested in sharing the details of her life with a local busybody:

> Lana sighed. Really, there was no way around her humiliation. She just had to barrel straight on through it, over and over.
>
> "I'm sorry, Dixie. I'm afraid that won't happen. The truth is … Graham moved out."
>
> Dixie narrowed her pale blue eyes and touched her hair again. "Why on earth would he do that?" she asked.
>
> It wasn't at all the reaction Lana was expecting, and it struck her as equally tragic and hilarious … The Mylar balloons swayed overhead in the man-made breezes of central air-conditioning while piped-in Rick Springfield crooned about wanting Jessie's girl, and Lana couldn't help but laughing at the horror of it all.

Dixie's reaction validates Lana's experiences somewhat, but it also pierces her "just trying to cope" bubble—and the pain seeps in, too. Yes, why would he leave her? She's a good person, a good mom, and a hard worker. This, coupled with the unexpected question, acts as a release valve on Lana's pent-up emotions. Dixie's reaction to her shows the reader just how complex Lana's feelings are without Lana having to flatly say or think so herself.

Interior Monologue Cues

A character's thoughts will demonstrate her state of emotion for a given experience. Keep in mind that thoughts often read like summary and can slow down the pace of your story. So while you can get away with having a character think a direct and straightforward feeling, it's still better to approach it obliquely.

Here's an example from Caroline Leavitt's novel *Is This Tomorrow*. It's 1956, and Jewish single mother Ava Lark and her son, Lewis, stick out in a neighborhood full of nuclear families and Christians. Twelve-year-old Lewis has only a couple of friends (other fatherless children), so he spends a lot of time with his own imagination and thoughts. Here Leavitt shows that Ava's anxieties are influencing her son, which manifests in his irrational fear of a Communist missile attack in his own suburban neighborhood:

> Lewis didn't feel like roaming the neighborhood anymore. A plane zoomed across the sky. Lewis looked up. He imagined Mr. Corcoran's missile flying down from the sky, aimed right at them, lean and silver as a needle. Would he see it before it struck or would it happen so fast that everything would be obliterated? Would he know a Communist if he saw one?

As a child, Lewis often misunderstands what he sees and hears, and his thoughts show us these distortions in ways that spoken words might not effectively convey.

Imagistic Cues

You can craft a visual analogy—a simile or stylized visual description—to convey emotion or experience. Consider this metaphoric one from Max Barry's dystopian thriller novel *Lexicon*, in which young adults on the fringes of society are trained to use powers of persuasion to force people to do their bidding, with terrible consequences. As the book opens, we meet a character named Wil who has clearly been through a traumatic event, but we don't yet know what has occurred:

> A door opened. On the other side of it was a world of stunted color and muted sound, as if something was stuck in Wil's ears, and eyes, and possibly brain. He shook his head to clear it, but the world grew dark and angry and would not stay upright.

Rather than rely on heavy exposition or backstory, Barry uses imagery to create a visceral experience of Wil's state of mind. It generates page-turning tension that makes you want to keep reading to find out what happens next, and it doesn't fall into flat, dull narrative summary.

These images, from Chuck Wendig's young adult fantasy novel *Under the Empyrean Sky* use analogies to convey emotion:

> His palms are slick with sweat, and his stomach has gone as sour as a cup of vinegar.

Writing the Intimate Character

He sits in his jail cell with that thought twisting in his mind like a worm trying to tie itself in knots.

Sometimes you can simply use a straightforward visual to communicate what a character is feeling. Here's a visual cue from Michael Faber's *The Book of Strange New Things*, in which a character shows sudden sadness in a scene when sadness is not otherwise evident:

He turned toward her darkened face again, and was alarmed to see teardrops twinkling on her jaw and in the corners of her mouth.

And here's a more metaphoric imagistic cue from *Love in the Time of Cholera* by Gabriel García Márquez that uses the sense of smell—the fumes of gold cyanide—to convey both literal death and the death of love:

Although the air coming through the window had purified the atmosphere, there still remained for the one who could identify it the dying embers of hapless love in the bitter almonds.

This snippet from Lidia Yuknavitch's *The Small Backs of Children* contains a more lyrical imagistic cue:

Her mother is a moon eye in the sky. Not perfectly white, but bruise-hued. The moon eye casts a gaze over all of the world, over violence and lovers with equal compassion, over living and dead, over children and old men curling into brittle-boned fetal positions in bed.

Keep a list of character cues close at hand whenever you sit down to write. While you might not use every cue in every scene—sometimes you'll need just a few—they are a crucial shorthand code by which you communicate to readers how your characters are feeling without overtly stating their emotions.

Character cues will never fail to build nuance and texture in your scenes. The more nuanced and layered your cues, the more complex and rounded your characters will seem, and the more compelling the tension will be in your story.

NOW YOU

SCOUR THE SURFACE

Whenever you're stuck on how your character feels in a scene, try this exercise: Write down the surface feeling at the top of a sheet of paper—for instance, fear. Then think for a few minutes about what other subset feelings are likely present; in this example, maybe hurt, loneliness, and yearning. Now ask: What cues can you use to convey these subset feelings?

Write a paragraph that uses each cue type. What dialogue would your character speak in this scene if her surface feeling is fear but her subset feelings are hurt, loneliness, and yearning? What physical action cues might she exhibit? Can you convey these emotions with imagistic cues or reactions from other characters?

DEMONSTRATE FEELINGS

It's typical in a manuscript to use variations on the verb *feel* to express emotion: *He felt mad. I feel scared.* While these practical expressions of feelings are not necessarily bad, you can invite your readers more deeply into the experiences of your characters by *demonstrating* those feelings. Try it now with the list of feeling prompts below (or feel free to comb through your own manuscript for the words *feel* or *felt*). Use one of the character cues discussed in this chapter to express the feeling without using versions of the verb *feel*. Hint: Avoid thoughts; stick to action, dialogue, and images.

- He felt sad to hear the news.
- She felt angry when he yelled at her.
- I had never felt so embarrassed before.
- You felt overwhelming desire.
- His expression made her feel afraid.
- Her words inspired a feeling of dread.
- I'd never feel joy again.
- You always feel sick.
- We never felt loved.

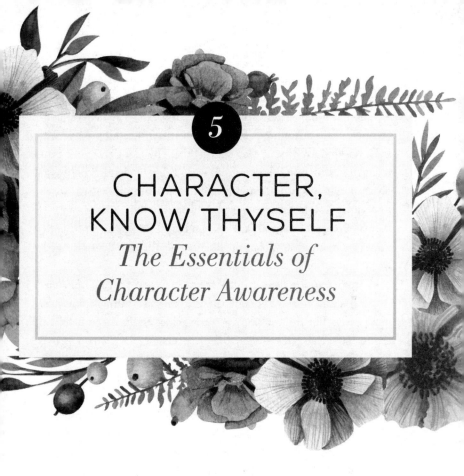

5

CHARACTER, KNOW THYSELF
The Essentials of Character Awareness

"Everything that irritates us about others can lead us to an understanding of ourselves."

—C.G. JUNG

Early drafts are an exercise in getting to know your character and her story—you are, in essence, telling the story to *yourself* first, so that you can figure out what to add or omit when fine-tuning the story for your readers. The more you learn about your character while drafting, the less you will be tempted to include unwieldy passages of backstory, advance "telegraphing"(in which you use summary to tell readers what a character is about to do or say through action and dialogue), or excessive passages of description in your final manuscript.

Though some writers are loathe to cut precious sentences, I encourage you to pen more pages and scenes starring your protagonist than you will ever use. I even suggest that you test-drive your protagonist in different scenarios and with different characters (possibly even ones who won't actually make an appearance in your story) to discover how he behaves in a variety of situations. Then, from the reams of pages at your fingertips, you can cull organic representations of your characters and reveal them fully through demonstrated words and actions.

If this isn't quite clear, think of the early stages of dating someone. When you first meet, you don't instantly know everything about this new person, but you get many powerful clues and cues—much like the essential character cues introduced in chapter four, which do the work of communicating emotions subtly. People reveal their biases, their wounds, their yearnings, and their temperament in every word and deed. People who have been abused might use carefully controlled language or have difficulty trusting others. People with deep empathy often focus on the emotions of others and might even feel what others are feeling. Those with deep religious underpinnings may see the divine in everything or openly discuss their spirituality.

The challenge to good character development is in seeing your characters as fully realized human beings, not just figments of your imagination. The best characters are so vivid that readers refuse to accept they don't exist outside the pages of a book. You can create characters this true to life by making sure they ring with authenticity and plausibility, and by avoiding the mistakes that stifle them.

Throughout this chapter we'll look at some bad habits to avoid when building strong characters. We'll also explore how to choose the right degree of reader-character intimacy, and how to create believable parameters of your character's self-knowledge.

AVOIDING MISSTEPS IN CHARACTER DEVELOPMENT

Let's look at some common pitfalls you should avoid when writing your character and strategies for avoiding them.

Steer Clear of Overt Self-Awareness at the Beginning

Strong characters should change over the time period of your story, and this change should result from the events and consequences they encounter at each of the major, transformative turning points in your plot (or *energetic markers*, which I discuss further in chapter twelve). Your protagonist should not be exactly the same at the end as she was at the beginning, and her change must be earned and believable. And while we want to follow a character we like and respect, you must allow room for her to grow; in other words, she can't start out perfect or too self-aware.

In the manuscripts I edit for clients, I frequently see protagonists who are hyper self-aware. These perfect people know their every motivation and never second-guess themselves. They are bastions of emotional maturity—in fact, they are practically self-help gurus. In fiction, this is a problem. Characters who seem to know themselves too well come off as narcissistic or in denial. Characters who are a little unsure, on the other hand, who have secrets in their past that they overcompensate for or try to hide, who are more self-deprecating than self-assured, win us over because they feel real.

Take this example from Tana French's mystery novel *The Secret Place*. In first-person POV, Dublin detective Stephen Moran reveals to readers that he's a guy who knows some things about himself but still makes decisions based on old wounds. He's working in Cold Cases, a department that handles nonactive murder cases:

> Cold Cases is good. Very bleeding good for a guy like me: working-class Dub, first in my family to go for a Leaving Cert instead of an apprenticeship. I was out of uniform by twenty-six, out of the

General Detective Unit and into Vice by twenty-eight—Holly's da put in a word for me there. Into Cold Cases the week I turned thirty, hoping there was no word put in, scared there was. I'm thirty-two now. Time to keep moving on up.

But later in the same scene, we see that Moran's statement "Cold Cases is good" may not be the whole truth; he is perhaps lying to himself a little bit or whitewashing over the reality:

> Seven years on, and the truth was starting to hit.
>
> Murder is the thoroughbred stable. Murder is a shine and a dazzle, a smooth ripple like honed muscle, take your breath away. Murder is a brand on your arm, like an elite army unit's, like a gladiator's, saying for all your life: *One of us. The finest.*
>
> I want Murder.

Moran is a man conflicted. On the one hand, he feels that he's lucky to have made it into Cold Cases, as he is clearly one of the few educated members of his working-class family. On the other hand, he wants to move up. Or at least he thinks he does. There's something about the Murder department that clearly has a seductive hold over him—he waxes poetic about it, after all, and yet, he's also scared of it, as evidenced by the line "… hoping there was no word put in, scared there was." In other words, Moran is a man who has a goal—to work for the Murder team—but he doesn't fully understand all the nuances of his motivation. He's a man with potential for growth and change. And the particular cold case he's working at the beginning of the novel, which teams him up with a detective from Murder, Antoinette Conway, will give him a good look at whether he truly wants what he thinks he wants.

Complexity is essential for developing characters. "I contain multitudes," says Walt Whitman in his famous poem "Song of Myself." So should your characters.

Here's another example of a perfectly imperfect character from Liane Moriarty's contemporary novel *Big Little Lies*. Madeline is a just-turned-forty mother of two girls: a teenager who is pushing Madeline away, and a kindergartner. This passage is Madeline's third-person intimate musing on the imperfections of age and mortality as she drives her daughter to school:

> As she drove the familiar route to the school, she considered her magnificent new age. Forty. She could still feel "forty" the way it felt when she was fifteen. Such a colorless age. Marooned in the middle of your life. Nothing would matter all that much when you were forty. …
>
> Madeline always had to do a minor shift in her head when she heard something on the news about a woman dying in her forties. *But wait, that could be me! That would be sad! People would be sad if I was dead! Devastated, even. So there, age-obsessed world. I might be forty, but I am cherished.*
>
> On the other hand, it was probably perfectly natural to feel sadder over the death of a twenty-year-old than a forty-year-old. The forty-year-old had enjoyed twenty more years of life. That's why, if there was a gunman on the loose, Madeline would feel obligated to throw her middle-aged self in front of the twenty-year-old. Take a bullet for youth. It was only fair.
>
> Well, she would, if she could be sure it was a nice young person. Not one of those insufferable ones, like the child driving the little blue Mitsubishi in front of Madeline.

Madeline's musings are full of complexity about her feelings on age, life, and whether she would genuinely "take a bullet for youth"—which she decides she would do only if the young person was nice. This scene is funny and human, and it clearly shows that Madeline is a person who doesn't have it all perfectly figured out, even at forty. Her complexities give her room to grow.

Let Go of Likability

There's been much debate about the likability of characters in fiction. The issue is so charged that authors Claire Messud and Jennifer Weiner took opposing opinions in op-ed pieces for *The Guardian* and *Slate* in 2013. Does a character have to be likable in order to keep readers turning pages? A more plausible goal is to craft sympathetic characters—that is, characters that readers can understand. Readers need to believe and relate to your characters' motivations, and they need to care enough about them to keep reading—but this isn't necessarily the same as *liking* a character. An outright mean or egocentric character might turn a reader off, but one who is going through a hard time and is therefore behaving a little badly, or one who has a justifiable reason to be cranky, annoyed, or aloof, is acceptable. The key, of course, is that your less-than-likable character changes and becomes aware of his behavior soon enough to begin making adjustments.

The POV you ultimately choose can also help you moderate this issue of likability. First person allows no real distance between your character and the reader, so if your character is struggling at the beginning, and prone to being less than likable, third-person intimate or omniscient might be a better choice.

At the beginning of Andrew Ervin's novel *Burning Down George Orwell's House*, written in third-person intimate, antihero Ray Welter has sold his soul to a resource-consuming corporation and has reluctantly divorced his wife. He's spending his last evilly earned money on a trip to the isolated Isle of Jura off the coast of Scotland, where George Orwell wrote his famous dystopian novel, *Nineteen Eighty-Four*. Ray is a broken man whose PR campaign single-handedly sold more gas-guzzling cars than the company ever had before, which caused layoffs in a small factory in his father's hometown and wrecked Ray's marriage in the process. By taking the trip to the Isle of Jura, he's essentially running away from his life because he has nothing left to lose. But he's also facing off with himself and taking responsibility for the damage he's caused. In the beginning, we don't necessarily like him so much as take pity on him as the natural world, and then Jura's residents, work against him:

> Even with the ferry nearing the shore, or the shore nearing the ferry, Ray still felt like he might never make it to Jura. Zeno's paradox would take over. He would continue to travel half the distance, and then half of that, and half of that, and. … The closer he got, the more he felt his body shutting down. Famine, dehydra-

tion, and fatigue nipped at his heels. Marshmallow-like mucus colonized his chest and bits of it escaped every time he coughed. ...

In a later scene, he meets the man who will drive him to his hotel:

"You can call me Mr. Pitcairn."

"It sounds like the whole island was expecting me, Mr. Pitcairn."

"The whole island? Who do you think you are, the king? Did you think we're one big happy family? That we were going to throw you a parade?"

These passages make us feel sorry for Ray, which helps to redeem a character who might not hold our sympathy otherwise. And, of course, Ray does evolve and change enough to earn our true compassion over time.

Don't Be Afraid to Embrace the Shadow

When you craft a character who is a little bit blind to her own imperfections and don't make her overly self-aware at the beginning, this allows you to introduce and work with a character flaw. This flaw serves as a kind of antagonist, tripping up your character along the way and creating both great tension and the beginnings of a character arc. Having a character overcome her flaws is a wonderful and necessary way to create change.

A flaw can range from stubbornness to denial to being overly optimistic when circumstances suggest otherwise. A flaw has to be big enough to cause conflict but small enough to be overcome by story's end. Famed psychoanalyst Carl Jung coined the term *shadow side* to refer to flaws that the character doesn't fully grasp about herself. This means that your protagonist doesn't always know that these flaws exist inside her, but she eventually will learn about them the hard way and will have to work to overcome them.

Keep in mind that bold, funny, intelligent people all have flaws—so the flaw doesn't have to be your protagonist's predominant trait but rather just an aspect of her character that causes trouble. Trouble, after all, is a hallmark of conflict.

Remember, too, that a flaw has to eventually transform into a strength, so don't give your character an irredeemable flaw like racist views or violent physical outbursts.

Avoid Self-Conscious or Overly Pointed Dialogue

Dialogue is such a versatile tool for providing revelation and information that it is abused as an inelegant means for introducing unwieldy plot points or hefty doses of backstory. In real life, people rarely sit down and parse out the nuances of their feelings in conversation unless they're in a therapy session or having a heart-to-heart, the latter of which you'll want to use sparingly (unless you're writing a romance novel). Save dialogue for communicating information that will drive the plot forward, reveal the truth of your character, or deliver new information about him.

Self-conscious dialogue doesn't ring true, as in this example:

> "I'm aloof because my parents withheld affection from me as a child," she said. "It really shaped me into being unable to trust people."

This dialogue is too on the nose. More likely, a character who received limited affection from her parents will simply behave in a way that shows she doesn't trust others. She might ask a lot of questions or be suspicious of the motives of other characters.

You might also mistakenly make your character's dialogue too pointed: "We're going to find the killer and bring him to justice!" she could say. While the words might be accurate, they might not be true to your character's personality, or it might not be necessary for her to announce this when the action has clearly dictated it.

It's also common in early drafting to erroneously use dialogue to fill in the gaps of narrative voice—that is, to have your character speak details that are unnecessarily cumbersome in dialogue and would be better left in the smooth summary of narrative. For example, it can get unwieldy to have a character describe her surroundings in dialogue:

"This room is so opulent. Look at those brocade curtains, with that elaborate design. And the tall bed with its heavy mahogany wood posts."

This setting description is delivered more neatly in the narrative voice:

She found the room opulent, with heavy brocade curtains woven with an elaborate Celtic design, and a four-poster bed made of gleaming, heavy mahogany.

What dialogue does best is reveal character's feelings and goals, and drive the action forward. When you're in the third-person intimate or omniscient POV, which are less intimate than first person, dialogue helps connect the reader to the real-time moment. Speaking aloud is something we do in the present moment—it is a form of action.

Diana Gabaldon's second novel in the Outlander series, *Dragonfly in Amber*, begins in the third-person intimate POV of a Scottish historian named Roger Wakefield. Notice how the energy of the scene brings it to life: We feel that we are *in* the scene, rather than watching it, when the author shifts from narrative voice to dialogue.

She was middle height and very pretty. He had an overall impression of fine bones and white linen, topped with a wealth of curly brown hair in a sort of half-tamed chignon. And in the middle of it all, the most extraordinary pair of light eyes, just the color of well-aged sherry.

The eyes swept up from his size-eleven plimsolls to the face a foot above her. The sidelong smile grew wider. "I hate to start right off with a cliché," she said, "but my, how you have grown, young Roger!"

Roger felt himself flushing. The woman laughed and extended a hand. "You are Roger, aren't you? My name's Claire Randall; I was an old friend of the Reverend's. But I haven't seen you since you were five years old."

Dialogue should always serve a purpose, and that purpose should not be to reveal something obvious to the reader. Here's a piece of advice worthy of repeating again and again: *Don't overexplain*. Remember that readers are savvy—they pick up on small body cues and imagery, and they read between the lines. You especially don't need to be obvious in dialogue. If anything, allowing for a little obscurity or nuance in dialogue, or a "tug-of-war" in which characters speak in opposition to each other, are better ways to keep readers engaged with the spoken words of your characters.

Though the previous excerpt is a section on dialogue, I'd be remiss if I didn't point out Gabaldon's clever use of a character cue. We get a clear picture in that scene that Roger is taller than Claire. But Roger does not self-describe as "very tall" or give his stated height. Gabaldon describes him thus: "The eyes swept up from his size-eleven plimsolls to the face a foot above her." Brilliantly handled, and subtle.

HOW CHARACTERS BECOME AWARE

Your protagonist won't stay flawed and in the dark forever—not if you want to create a believable plot and compelling characters. Over the course of your book, her flaw will slowly become a strength through challenges and clashes with antagonists, but also through developing relationships with allies and romantic partners. You could liken a protagonist to a seed; when stress is applied to the seed and the hard outer shell cracks open, only then can the seedling germinate—a tiny tendril of growth slowly burgeoning into beautiful fruition.

The key to believable characterization is *subtlety.* You don't want to suddenly turn your shy character into the life of the party in the middle of your novel. Instead, give her a voice and a presence in increments, and make the change noticeable by story's end. Likewise, if your character is stubborn at the beginning, he shouldn't become the most flexible guy on earth by the end; he should put that stubbornness to good use for a cause or learn to take a few steps out of his stubborn zone for love. And when it comes to character self-awareness, you shouldn't write characters into big, dramatic epiphanies about themselves. Once again, you should rely on words and deeds—dialogue and actions—to convey how they have changed.

Writing the Intimate Character

Let's look at a few examples of characters who are coming to a new understanding of themselves.

In Claire Kells's novel *Girl Underwater*, protagonist Avery Delacorte survived a plane crash with one member of her swim team and three small children. In the months since she was rescued and returned home, she has been cocooned by shock and denial of the events that took place, trying to regain her life and her ability to swim. She spends a good portion of the book avoiding Colin Shea, with whom she was stranded, and for whom she has feelings she doesn't want to admit. He is the touchstone for her painful memories of the crash, and she is afraid that too much time with him will awaken them all. But as the book unfolds, through interactions with others and the healing she does in therapy, she slowly unfurls. Toward the end of the book, she runs into Colin:

> As before, it takes me a while to reconcile the memory of Colin Shea to the reality of him. I always expect the worst: flashbacks, regret, unbearable tension. Instead, it's relief that sweeps through me—relief and a strange sense of groundedness.
>
> "Better weather up here?" He watches me for a moment, perhaps gauging my reaction to his teasing tone, his shy smile. I see then that he's changed in other ways, too—he seems relaxed, eased of some terrible burden. I don't know if that burden is the crash, or expectations, or even me, but its absence plays on his face.

Kells doesn't have Avery come to a dramatic "I am healed" epiphany, but it is evident that her wounds have mended enough to not only be in Colin's presence but to feel relief in it. The subtle use of physical cues in this passage show this change, and even the way Avery interprets Colin's mood—that he seems "eased of some terrible burden"—says as much about her as it does about him.

When in doubt over what knowledge your character should have about his motivations, err on the side of less, particularly in the first half of your novel. In chapter twelve, we'll talk about ways to introduce one new point of awareness at each major plot juncture. Be sure that your characters act and speak first, and think second. The more intimate your point of view, the less need for revelations of character. The less intimate your point of view, the more room you have to explain.

Most important of all, consider that if you reveal too much too soon in a story, you are likely to lose your readers altogether. One of the most powerful ways to keep readers reading is to create a bit of mystery—leaving questions unanswered so that readers have no choice but to keep turning pages to find out what's next.

NOW YOU

CHARACTER IN ADVERSITY

Put your character in a scene where adversity leads him to an epiphany about himself that he finds unpleasant: realizing that he isn't very strong, that he's more selfish than he imagined, etc. Ideally, put him in a scene with other characters who push or test him.

THE FLAWED PERSON

Write a monologue in your character's voice, in first person, in which she describes all of her worst habits and flaws, dark secrets, and quirks. Then switch to third person and have her describe her best qualities, what people like about her, and her virtues and strengths. Notice if she comes across as more or less self-aware depending on the POV, as well as likable or sympathetic.

6

TIGHTEN TENSION
*Tricks for Tension-Building
in Each Point of View*

> *"When you create in your reader an
> unconscious apprehension, anxiety,
> worry, question, or uncertainty, then
> the reader will unconsciously seek to
> relieve that uneasiness."*

—DONALD MAASS, LITERARY AGENT

Writers are always trying to capture, create, and tighten the elusive quality known as *tension* in their fiction. When readers can't stop reading, when the story pulls them along by an ever-tightening rope, you've generated tension in your story. In truth, many different ingredients go into the pot to create tension, and just as many bad habits can kill it. In this chapter we'll look at the different ways to keep tension taut within the limits of each point of view.

CREATING TENSION IN FIRST PERSON

When writing in the first-person POV, the line between readers and the character is slim at most. First person is like stepping into a holographic experience of a character's life. Because of the nature of the human mind, the more you read the word *I*, the more the experiences of the character begin to feel like your own. But the intimacy created by first person can also prove a challenge when trying to create tension. Here are some ways to do so successfully.

Let Other Characters Carry the Mystery

First person allows you to see the machinery of the character at work—readers witness firsthand when your character is fooled or misled, or when he jumps into a bad situation despite his better judgment. You cannot pull the wool over your readers' eyes so easily, because the character can't hide much.

Unfortunately, putting all your cards on the table, so to speak, is not an effective tension technique. Tension relies upon sleight of hand and mystery, a sense of questions left unanswered. So how do you keep that mystery alive when the character is spilling her every sense and thought into the reader's mind?

One way to handle this issue is to let other characters carry or create mystery for the protagonist. While readers do know your protagonist's every thought and feeling, they don't know the thoughts and motivations of co-characters and antagonists.

Here's an example from Krassi Zourkova's novel *Wildalone*, in which Thea, a prodigy violinist studying at Princeton, has been doggedly pursued by an enigmatic, handsome, and moody man named Rhys, who courts her furiously but refuses to answer many of her

Writing the Intimate Character

questions. In the following scene, he takes her to an undisclosed location without telling her why. As you can see, the tension builds as Thea begins to wonder if she has made a foolish mistake by accompanying this near-stranger:

> The automatic locks clicked. I tried to think of something else, to act as if I hadn't just driven off with a guy I barely knew. Rita and all her talk about stalking! This was Princeton, everyone knew the place was safer than a police station. Besides, if I wanted a safe and sheltered life, what was I doing in a foreign country, all by myself? …
>
> Before I noticed, the houses had given way to woods. Smudged green, racing on both sides of the road.
>
> "Where are you taking me?"
>
> A smile—slow and sure of its impact. For a moment or two, while my heart pounded its panic through my chest, I had mental flashes of what could happen next. Things this guy might do to me. Stuff I had seen only in movies.
>
> He stepped on the brakes and swerved into the grass. I looked in the side mirror—the road was completely empty.
>
> Was there any chance that pain hurt less if inflicted by someone beautiful?
>
> A key turned, choking the engine off—
>
> Then everything became absolutely quiet.

Thea's feelings are transparent throughout the scene—we know exactly how she's feeling because she narrates each moment as her anxiety builds to panic. But we don't know what's going on in Rhys's mind, what he has planned, and whether he has diabolical intentions. He holds the mystery, which keeps the tension high. When your character doesn't know what is happening or what will happen, or when she distrusts another character, this creates instant tension. While you can use this technique in any POV, it's especially effective in first person, where the level of intimacy leaves little room for uncertainty.

Make Your Character a "Fish out of Water"

Most great plots follow the universal story structure, which I discuss in more depth in chapter twelve. Every story that follows this model contains a point where your character feels like an outsider or a "fish out of water." This usually occurs just after the Point of No Return (often called the inciting incident), when your character takes a leap from his ordinary and familiar world or reality into a new or exotic one. But there are multiple places in a story where you can show your character feeling out of place, especially as he grows stronger and gathers more courage. Newfound strength and resolve can encourage a character to try new things and interact with new people.

In first person, "fish out of water" scenes provide a wonderful opportunity for tension because they force the character to behave outside of his comfort zone, while allowing access and insight into his internal perceptions. This enables you to show this clash of expectation versus reality, and of the familiar versus the unfamiliar.

Here's an example from Diana Gabaldon's *Dragonfly in Amber*. In this scene, Claire, the twentieth-century accidental time traveler, has returned to 1740s France with her Scottish husband, Jamie Fraser. Claire is already a fish out of water because she is from the future, but her outsider status is increased because she is also far from her quiet life in the Scottish countryside. The French court is a wild and bawdy place, and the reserved and highly monogamous Claire is not quite prepared when Jamie introduces her to the king and his scantily clad mistress:

> I dipped automatically, struggling to keep my eyes on the floor and wondering where I would look when I bobbed up again. Madame Neslé de la Tourelle was standing just behind Louis, watching the introduction with a slightly bored look on her face. Gossip said that "Neslé" was Louis's current favorite. She was, in current vogue, wearing a gown cut *below* both breasts, with a bit of supercedent gauze which was clearly meant for the sake of fashion, as it couldn't possibly function for either warmth or concealment.

It was neither the gown nor the prospect it revealed that had rattled me, though. The breasts of "Neslé"... were further adorned with a pair of nipple jewels that caused their settings to recede into insignificance ...

I rose, red-faced and coughing, and managed to excuse myself, hacking politely into a handkerchief as I backed away.

Not all tension must be negative, scary, or anxiety-inducing. As this passage demonstrates, putting a character in a situation she doesn't know how to handle, and which threatens her own sensibilities, holds the reader's attention quite effectively and injects a little humor.

CREATING TENSION IN THIRD-PERSON INTIMATE

Third-person intimate, I will continue to say, shares many similarities with first person, though that tiny beat of distance it offers by using the pronouns *he* or *she* does seem to create a gap between the reader and the emotional impact. You must always be aware, as well, that the *he/she* pronouns have a way of lending themselves to tangents and asides you want to be careful to avoid. Here are ways to use third-person intimate to its fullest tension, even when emotions are at a distance.

Drop into the Action

At one time or another, most writers have fallen into the bad habit of offering several pages of backstory about a character's life. But remember that long passages of summary separated from narrative voice will drain tension and slow your story's pace. Tension remains at its highest when you drop right into the action *en medias res* (Latin for "in the midst of things"), without explanation, particularly at the beginnings of scenes and chapters.

In this scene from Caroline Leavitt's literary novel *Is This Tomorrow*, set in 1956, twelve-year-old Lewis is supposed to meet up with his best friend, Jimmy. On the way, a group of older bullies intercepts him, and he is forced to hide with the help of Jimmy's sister, Rose. While in hiding, Lewis falls asleep outside and misses meeting Jimmy. When he gets home, the following action unfolds in the point of view of his mother, Ava, who is something of a neighborhood pariah for being both divorced and Jewish. She is also the last person to have seen Jimmy:

> "Jimmy's not here?" Lewis said. Ava stared at him, incredulous. His hair was awry and there was some sort of muddy stain splashed across his shirt and pants.
>
> "Weren't you with your brother?" Dot cried, and Rose looked down at the ground. "Where is he?"
>
> Ava felt Jake's hand against the small of her back. She thought of Jimmy, crying because he had lost at checkers. She saw him standing at his doorstep, waving at her, his chin tilted up. Jimmy, she thought. Oh Jesus, Jimmy.
>
> The cops milled around, asking questions. "We should do a search," one of the neighbors said, and a cop lifted one hand. "Now, just settle down and let us do our job," he snapped. "Things need to be done quickly and in the right way and you can do more harm than good if you interfere."

Leavitt lets the action do the talking and keeps the internal monologue to a minimum, which maintains the high level of tension.

Use Specific Sensory Details

In third person, readers are at a slightly greater distance than in first person. When it comes to what the protagonist feels, they are passengers along for the ride instead of inhabitants in the protagonist's head. In this case it's better to use specific sensory details and imagery to draw the reader into the character's sensory realm of her bodily experience and emotions. Specific details invoke all the senses. If a woman is walking through a park in autumn, then we should *smell* the peculiar perfume of mulch and ozone in the air and *hear* the crunch of dry leaves beneath her boots and the trilling of a particular bird. We should *feel* the precise crispness of air on her face. Specific sensory details also focus the lens, so to speak, and draw the reader's attention to an important moment in the scene, which increases the tension.

In Liane Moriarty's *Big Little Lies*, Celeste is a well-kept housewife and the mother of twin sons. She's the kind of woman whom other women in her circle judge as "perfect." They see her as the woman who has it all: gorgeous, with a handsome husband, a wealthy lifestyle, and two healthy children. But there's a dark side to Celeste's story, and it's revealed slowly, doled out with care for maximum mystery and tension through powerful and beautiful sensory details. In this scene, Celeste walks with her sons and husband through the schoolyard. What should be a normal scene of a picture-perfect family begins to warp at the edges as Celeste describes every detail. The reader starts to wonder if Celeste is revealing darker information in these tiny, sensory sound bytes:

> It was one of those days. It had been a while. Not since well before Christmas. Celeste's mouth was dry and hollow. Her head throbbed gently. She followed the boys and Perry through the school yard with her body held stiffly, carefully, as if she were a tall fragile glass in danger of spilling.
>
> She was hyperaware of everything: the warm air against her bare arms, the straps of her sandals in between her toes, the edges of the leaves of the Moreton Bay fig tree, each sharply delineated against the blue of the sky. It was similar to that intense way you felt when you were newly in love, or newly pregnant, or driving a car on your own for the first time. Everything felt significant.
>
> "Do you and Ed fight?" she'd asked Madeline once.
>
> "Like cats and dogs," Madeline had said cheerfully.
>
> Celeste could somehow tell she was talking about something else entirely.

This passage contains lots of telling details. Celeste's mouth is "dry and hollow," and she holds her body "stiffly" as if she were "a tall fragile glass in danger of spilling." She is "hyperaware" as she slows down and notices the world around her. These details alert the reader that something has happened to Celeste—something bad. Maybe she's ill.

Maybe someone has died. The truth is hinted at more clearly when she remembers asking her friend Madeline if she fights with her husband. That Madeline can answer "cheerfully" tells Celeste that other people do not fight the way she and her own husband do. Other women's husbands don't hit them.

If Moriarty had simply chosen to write a straightforward passage— "Perry had hit her again"—it wouldn't have had the same effect. Notice the calculated focus the sensory details draw into the light, allowing the painful truth to sneak up on the reader. This is tension at its finest.

CREATING TENSION IN OMNISCIENT

Omniscient POV is the all-knowing historian or godlike lens, in which the narrative voice draws on information the characters don't know and can leap in and out of the minds of different characters as needed. It lends itself to the least amount of intimacy and thus has a greater propensity for summary language that explains information to the reader. You also run the risk of zooming the camera in and out at dizzying speed, abusing the leeway that omniscient provides. Precisely because you have so much room in omniscient, you have to be careful not to yank readers all over the place, which will kill tension by confusing them.

Narrow the Lens

A great way to create tension in omniscient is to purposely start out at a distance—from an external, all-knowing vantage point—and then narrow your lens to an ever closer, more intimate, and internal vantage point by homing in on the events, sensory details, and emotions of a specific scene.

Here's a great example from Gina Frangello's literary novel *A Life in Men*. In this scene, Mary and Nix, best friends and college girls who are vacationing in Greece, are taken to a villa and held against

Writing the Intimate Character

their will by two handsome Greek men they meet at a bar. The scene starts out in the big-picture omniscient voice and then condenses, focusing on the action in Nix's POV. Notice how the scene brims with tension. We feel unable to look away; we have to know what happens next.

> Two blonde girls stand on the balcony of a beautiful Cliffside Greek villa. They are perched too high above the winding road to escape by jumping, and any passerby would probably not understand English if they shouted, *Help!* Nix and Mary would appear simply to be admiring the pretty view—which is exactly what they are pretending to do while Titus and Zorg mix cocktails in the kitchen. The two men are evidently unconcerned about leaving them alone, confident that there is no means of escape.
>
> Nix feels as though she has landed in the middle of a play, one of those old-fashioned ones in which the characters are all in disguise and are saying things that don't mean what they seem to mean. Zorg is playing the part of cohost, smiling and mixing drinks as though he has not brought two women here against their will. For their part, the girls are acting like gracious guests, oohing and aahing at the view, asking for drinks they do not want so that they can have a moment alone together. …

We start out at a distance, outside the characters, as indicated by the sentences "Two blonde girls stand on a balcony ..." and "They are perched too high above the winding road to escape ..." While those sentences invoke some tension, it's not until Frangello drops deeply within Nix's point of view—"Nix feels as though she has landed in the middle of a play"—that the author begins to evoke real emotions. Frangello employs this technique at several other junctures throughout the book, pulling back for just a few paragraphs to give us the lay of the land and then diving in painfully close.

You can also employ the tension techniques for first person and third person when writing in the omniscient POV, particularly using sensory details and creating uncertainty.

Don't Forget Your Sentences

Often we're so busy constructing characters, scenes, and plots that we forget about the magic of the sentences themselves. Friction and alliteration create tension within the language, while lack of variety can deflate it. Sentences that are all the same length stack up to create a monotone or static quality. Too many sentences that begin with the same word can also create a lackluster reading experience.

Language is, at its best, musical, rhythmic, and energetic. Your sentences, therefore, don't have to merely describe characters and events—they can be symphonies of their own making.

Of course, this topic could constitute an entire book. But for our purposes, just look at the following lovely, interesting, tense sentences—full of strong verbs, alliteration, poetic imagery, and more—and then "listen" to the way your own sentences flow. Reading your work aloud can help with this endeavor. Notice in these passages how the authors use word choice, imagery juxtaposed with other imagery, analogies, strong verbs, or well-positioned adjectives to best effect. Notice, too, how each passage makes you want to read more.

From *A Visit from the Goon Squad* by Jennifer Egan:

> The gold landed on the coffee's milky surface and spun wildly. Bennie was mesmerized by this spinning, which he took as evidence of the explosive gold-coffee chemistry. A frenzy of activity that had mostly led him in circles: wasn't that a fairly accurate description of lust?

Here we have strong visuals that literally conjure the sense of sight: "gold," "coffee," "a milky surface." For a short passage, there's a lot of action in the verbs: "spun wildly," "frenzy of activity." In my favorite part of the passage, she compares all this gold-coffee-milk action to the "chemistry" of lust, which is metaphorically compelling.

From *Cloud Atlas* by David Mitchell:

> Over an hour later London shunted itself southward, taking the Curse of the Brothers Hoggins with it. Commuters, these hapless

souls who enter a lottery of death twice daily on Britain's decrepit railways, packed the dirty train.

This passage not only has some wonderful words you don't hear all the time, such as the verb *shunted* and the adjective *decrepit* but it also rings with the poetry of alliteration, which is when words begin or end with similar sounds. If you read the sentences aloud, you hear the soft shushing of "shunted" and "southward" and the hard *C* of "Curse" and "Commuters,"—and there is musicality in the way the hard and soft sounds brush up against one another. This passage also has a wonderful wry quality, which makes you both laugh and shudder.

From *Love in the Time of Cholera* by Gabriel García Márquez:

> As opposed to what his corpulence might suggest, Lotario Thugut had the rosebud genitals of a cherub, but this must have been a fortunate defect, because the most tarnished birds argued over who would have the chance to go to bed with him, and then they shrieked as if their throats were being cut, shaking the buttresses of the palace and making its ghosts tremble in fear.

The tension in this wonderful passage can again be found in word choice and startling imagery. How often do you hear the word *corpulence*, which is dripping with onomatopoeia (where a word sounds like what it is or does)? Then there are "tarnished birds," "buttresses," and my favorite for its shock value, "rosebud genitals." You get the feeling that García Márquez chose every word with keen intention.

From *Bel Canto* by Ann Patchett:

> Her heart was stuttering in her chest. The rush of her blood made a roar in her ears. What she heard when she strained to listen was the voice of the saint. "Now or never," Saint Rose told her. "I am with you only for this moment."

Here, the action of her words evokes a physical tension in the reader. We sense this character is nervous, that something intense is happening to her. Again, this is an example of demonstrating rather than lecturing to the reader. Patchett could have written, "she was anxious," but instead she shows it in crisp, careful language.

Tension is ultimately an element with many moving parts—the more you wield several tension-producing techniques at once in a scene, the more you will bring your writing, and your characters, to life.

NOW YOU

MILK THE MYSTERY

Write a scene in which a character is trying to discover something that is vital to the plot and, ideally, has high stakes. Depending on which POV you've selected, pick one of the techniques recommended in this chapter to keep the tension high. For example, if you're in first person, let another character hold the mystery, or make the character a "fish out of water."

CLICHÉ BUSTER

Tension at the sentence level is just as important as tension in a scene. Writers often kill tension by using clichés—words and phrases so familiar that they have become redundant, sentimental, or overused. Comb through your own manuscript for clichés and "freshen them" (in other words, find a new way to say what the cliché is saying), or choose clichés from this list to rewrite:

- Sweet as pie
- Pure as the driven snow
- The apple of my eye
- Absence makes the heart grow fonder.
- Bent out of shape
- Paled in comparison
- He was all thumbs.
- Jack of all trades
- A fly on the wall
- Let sleeping dogs lie.
- Live and learn.

Writing the Intimate Character

- She was a loose cannon.
- Passed with flying colors
- A picture is worth a thousand words.
- Rosebud lips
- Let's play it by ear.
- They didn't see eye to eye.
- Shoot from the hip.
- It's either sink or swim.
- I had to walk on eggshells.

PART TWO

*Character Cues and
Point of View*

7

BEHIND THE *I*
First-Person Point of View

> "... *What happens is of little significance*
> *compared with the stories we tell ourselves*
> *about what happens. Events matter little,*
> *only stories of events affect us.*"
>
> **—RABIH ALAHMEDDINE**

First-person POV has come into greater usage in contemporary literature. Perhaps our culture's obsession with selfies, social media, and reality television, in which we are given close and personal access to people's experiences and opinions, has sharpened audiences' hunger for this closeness in fiction. Many writers find they enjoy writing this point of view more than others because of its immediacy and intimacy, and readers enjoy reading it for the same reason.

When you write from the pronoun *I*, readers get to feel as though they are inside your viewpoint character's perspective. First person is perhaps the most intimate of the commonly used viewpoints; one can argue that only second person is more intimate. It is also the POV that gives the fullest *internal* snapshot of your characters. It's very immediate, making events feel as though they're happening *right now, right here.*

If you want to put a little emotional distance between your readers and your characters—perhaps if the characters are experiencing something traumatic or disturbing—you may opt to use a less-intimate POV. On the other hand, there is no better POV than first person for planting your readers in an experience that might otherwise be hard to explain or describe.

When writing in the first person, your viewpoint character must be present in each scene, and you are limited to only that character's POV until you switch to a new scene or chapter. This means that readers can know only what your character knows. For most writers this is not a problem, since limiting knowledge is a great way to build tension.

In chapter four I discussed the surface and subset emotions that broaden a character's personality and add depth, like a palette of colors that can be used to paint a clear and vivid emotional experience. Let's now look at how these emotions play out in the first-person POV and what cues can be employed to demonstrate them.

USING SURFACE AND SUBSET EMOTIONS IN FIRST PERSON

In first person you might have your character say, "I felt sad," or "I was angry," but this is the least effective way to demonstrate emotions in this POV. When a character simply states how she is feeling, this asks the reader to take the character's word for it. Demonstrating emotion through character cues offers proof to which a reader can viscerally relate.

Here's a snippet from Andrew Sean Greer's genre-bending literary science fiction novel, *The Impossible Lives of Greta Wells*. A traumatic incident sends the protagonist, Greta, to get electroshock therapy, which then shunts her out of her own time and into two other parallel lives, each in a different time, each containing a different version of her own life. I believe Greer chose first person because it is important that readers be firmly planted inside Greta's mind each time she passes into a parallel life, with close access to her emotional and sensory experiences. We need to stay close to her so we don't become confused. Notice how, right away, he demonstrates her emotion, not in telling language but in sensory description and her words and actions:

> Ruth took my hand. "Come now darling."
>
> But I could not move, watching him walking away from me, chatting with his companion and laughing, disappearing into the crowd.
>
> I felt her tight grip on me. Her concerned whisper: "Greta? Are you all right?"
>
> "I know that man," I said, pointing where he had been, a shimmer in the moonlight. I felt tears well in my eyes. "They're alive," was all I could say. "They didn't die."

How does Greta feel? To find the answer, let's look at the cues:

- **PHYSICAL ACTION CUE:** "I could not move." Here, it's what she *can't* do that hints at her emotion. Feeling paralyzed from action is often a sign of fear or sorrow.
- **SENSORY CUE:** "I felt tears well in my eyes." We all know the sensation of our eyes welling with tears, which makes this sensory cue especially relatable.
- **DIALOGUE CUE:** "'They're alive,' was all I could say. 'They didn't die.'" Only a surprised person would proclaim, "They're alive," so this spoken statement conveys shock.
- **OTHER CHARACTERS' REACTIONS:** We can take a cue from Ruth's response to Greta: "Are you all right?" This is a character reaction cue expressed in dialogue.

These cues all add up to the surface feeling, which might be *sadness*. But the subset feelings may include a range of emotions, including shock, relief, awe, and surprise.

In another scene from Greer's novel we find a few other cues:

> Then something rash and ridiculous occurred to me. I put my purse on my lap—a funny lumpy piece of leather—found the catch, searched through its handkerchiefs and lipsticks, and there it was. A pack of Pall Malls. I pulled one out and lit it with a match, and enjoyed the taste of death that no one here suspected. Oh, I deserved that little pleasure. What a wonderful world I had entered!

Here we have the following cues to the character's emotion and state of mind:

- **INTERIOR MONOLOGUE CUE:** Most of this passage contains only the character's thoughts. She has gone back in time to 1941, before anyone knew of the dangers of cigarette smoking, and she is marveling at the freedom this allows her to peacefully savor this frowned-upon luxury. In her modern world in the 1980s, she had quit smoking for her boyfriend because he insisted it was not good for her health.
- **IMAGE CUES:** She uses the image "enjoyed the taste of death," which is a metaphor for how the cigarettes cause illness, but the flip and playful tone of the description conveys that she's not terribly worried about her health, and that she misses the pleasure of her vice.

These cues add up to surface feelings of joy or pleasure, and a subset feeling of mischievousness, of getting away with something. These kinds of cues tell us a lot about the character without needing her to flatly state, "I felt mischievous," or "I missed smoking."

In the first-person POV, even though the character speaks in *I* statements, the writer still uses *cues* to demonstrate feelings rather than rely on expository statements that lack tension or drama.

INTRODUCING CHARACTERS IN FIRST PERSON

In first person you might be tempted to have your character introduce himself directly to the reader in a sort of monologue: "I'm a janitor by day who paints by night." You can use this method if you keep it brief, but a more effective way to introduce a character in the first person is, again, to rely on cues.

Here's an example from David Mitchell's science fiction novel, *The Bone Clocks*, in which we're first introduced to Holly Sykes, a teenager in England:

> I fling open my bedroom curtains, and there's the thirsty sky and the wide river full of ships and boats and stuff, but I'm already thinking of Vinny's chocolaty eyes, shampoo down Vinny's back, beads of sweat on Vinny's shoulders, and Vinny's sly laugh, and by now my heart's going mental and, God, I wish I was waking up at Vinny's place in Peacock Street and not in my own stupid bedroom. Last night, the words just said themselves, "Christ, I really love you, Vin," and Vinny puffed out a cloud of smoke and did this Prince Charles voice, "One must say, one's frightfully partial to spending time with you, too, Holly Sykes," and I nearly weed myself laughing, though I was a bit narked he didn't say "I love you too" back.

What are the cues that tell us things about Holly's emotional state, about who she is?

- **IMAGE CUES:** "Thirsty sky" and "chocolaty eyes," Holly's heart going "mental"—these images paint a picture of someone who is emotionally demonstrative, perhaps a bit of a dreamer or a poet, likely a young person. This is not a person who keeps her feelings hidden.
- **INTERIOR MONOLOGUE CUES:** Her interior monologue, or thoughts, are presented in an active way—as part of her observation of recent events. The focus of her thoughts is Vinny, a man or boy whose place she wishes she was "waking up at." This sounds

like a girl in love, no? Not to mention that the way her thoughts move, in a fluid, run-on sentence style, suggests that she is deeply immersed in her feelings; her thought patterns themselves reflect her emotional state.

- **DIALOGUE CUES:** She recounts telling Vinny in dialogue what she felt: "Christ, I really love you, Vin."

All of this adds up to a picture of a young, heartsick girl prone to big displays of emotion. Never once did she have to say, "I'm melodramatic," or "I'm lovesick."

OBSERVING THE SETTING IN FIRST PERSON

When revealing the setting in first person, you don't have the freedom afforded by the third-person or omniscient viewpoints to wander off-stage, away from your character. Every thought, perception, and observation must be filtered *through* your character's mind, heart, and senses. In other words, you must describe the setting as your character interacts with it rather than through exposition. To be frank, the former is much more effective—how your characters view the setting tells us a lot about them.

Let's use an example from Tana French's novel *The Secret Place*. Detective Stephen Moran, who works in Cold Cases but really wants to move up to the Murder department, has just been presented with a clue that would reopen a cold case. He takes it to Antoinette Conway, who works in Murder, in the hopes that she'll let him work on the case with her. In this scene, they first lay eyes on the girls' private school where they must conduct their investigation:

> I started to ask something, but Conway spun the car into a turn— so sudden, no blinker, I almost missed the moment we crossed over: high black-iron gates, stone guardhouse, iron arch with "St. Kilda College" picked out in gold. Inside the gates she braked. Let me take a good look.

The driveway swung a semicircle of white pebbles around a gentle slope of clipped green grass that went on forever. At the top of the slope was the school.

Someone's ancestral home, once, someone's mansion with grooms holding dancing carriage horses, with tiny-waisted ladies drifting arm in arm across the grass. Two hundred years old, more? A long building, soft gray stone, three tall windows up and more than a dozen across. A portico held up by slim curl-topped columns; a rooftop balustrade, pillars curved delicate as vases. Perfect, it was; perfect, everything balanced, every inch. Sun melting over it, slow as butter on toast.

What do Moran's observations about the school's physical setting tell us about his feelings and perceptions of it? Let's begin with the line "almost missed the moment we crossed over." Why would it matter if he missed the moment they passed through the gates? Because Moran holds this school, and the wealth and privilege it stands for, in great esteem; it represents status to him that he would like to obtain. This perception is bolstered by his attention to the details of the school, which take on a romantic air. He muses that it was once "someone's mansion," and he imagines "tiny-waisted ladies drifting arm in arm. ..." Moran's awe for this place is capped by this thought: "Perfect, it was; perfect, everything balanced, every inch."

Contrast it with Conway, who is completely unimpressed. She tells Moran: "This is the only time I'm sorry I'm a cop. When I see a shit-pile like this and I can't petrol-bomb it to f-ck."

Descriptions of setting should always be connected to the character's feelings about them. In first-person point of view, we should be unable to escape the character's feelings because we are *inside* his head.

UTILIZING SENSORY PERCEPTIONS IN ACTION IN FIRST PERSON

If books were comprised only of characters standing around thinking, feeling, and observing, no one would keep reading. Eventually, things must happen inside your story, and it must be clear to the reader through whose eyes we are seeing these events unfold. One scene could be retold from many different viewpoints and would be different each time because each character has unique, separate internal experiences and emotions, as well as her own set of stakes and consequences that is attached to the outcome of the event. Sensory perceptions are what allow readers to participate in the action with your characters. When readers feel, see, smell, hear, and taste what the characters do, the readers are right there with them.

In Sarah Waters's historical romance *Tipping the Velvet*, Nan is a young, aspiring actress in nineteenth-century London. She's been an admirer of a particular show, and even more so of a particular actress, Kitty, for some time. When circumstances allow her to become part of the show, and to eventually perform with Kitty for the first time, it's a very momentous night for Nan—it changes the course of her fate in two profound ways that turn the plot in a new direction. Waters places us in the thick of Nan's viewpoint by offering a full sensory experience.

In the following scene, Nan is onstage for the first time. As the action unfolds, notice how her sensory perceptions help us feel as though we are onstage with her. I've italicized sensory phrases to call them out:

> At first, so *blinded* was I by the lights, *I couldn't see the crowd at all*; I could only hear it, *rustling and murmuring—loud, and close*, it seemed, on every side. When at last I stepped for a second out of the glare of lime, and saw all the faces that were turned my way, I almost faltered and lost my place—and would have done, I think, had not Kitty at that moment *pressed my arm and murmured*, "We have them! Listen!" under cover of the orchestra. I did listen then—and realized that, unbelievably, she was right: there were *claps and friendly shouts*; there was *a rising hum of expectant pleasure* as we worked towards our chorus; there was, finally *a bubbling cascade of cheers and laughter* from gallery to pit.

Keep in mind that point of view is the camera through which readers "see" your story. If you are using first person, then they are able to see the action only as it unfolds within one character's experience at a time. Though Kitty is present in this scene, the author wouldn't jump suddenly from Nan's POV to Kitty's without a scene or chapter break.

WEAVING THOUGHT AND ACTION IN FIRST PERSON

First-person POV is like having a front-row seat at the thought concert in someone's head: You hear everything he thinks, which can, at times, get overwhelming. It's also easy to get lost in your character's thoughts and forget to keep the action moving. It's really just a matter of balance, of asking yourself whether the reader needs to know the thoughts that are going through your character's head at this point in time. To create balance, you should weave in thoughts with other kinds of scene elements, such as action and dialogue.

In Gillian Flynn's mystery novel *Sharp Objects*, protagonist Camille Preaker is a detective sent to investigate a case of missing girls in her hometown of Wind Gap, Missouri. It's a small town, and Camille has done everything she can to get as far from it, and her family, as possible. Going home is a complicated situation for her. In this scene, she goes into the woods where the body of one girl, Ann, was found. Thoughts and memories are juxtaposed with action:

> I sat down at the edge of the creek, running my palms over the rocky soil. Picked up a smooth, hot stone and pressed it against my cheek. I wondered if Ann had ever come here when she was alive. Maybe the new generation of Wind Gap kids had found more interesting ways to kill summers. When I was a girl, we swam at a spot just downstream where huge table rocks made shallow pools. Crawdads would skitter around our feet and we'd jump for them, scream if we actually touched one.

This scene deftly blends present-time action ("I sat down at the edge of the creek …. Picked up a smooth, hot stone,") with more passive memories ("When I was a girl, we swam at a spot just downstream … ."). But even Camille's memories are active, which results in thoughts that hum with energy.

In a later scene she stumbles across another girl's body:

> The blood hit my face fast, and a shimmer of sweat quickly covered my skin. My legs and arms went slack, and for a second I thought I might smack the ground right next to the woman, who was now quietly praying. I backed up, leaned against a parked car, and put my fingers to my neck, willing my thumping pulse to slow. My eyes picked up images in meaningless flashes: The grimy rubber tip of the old man's cane. A pink mole on the back of the woman's neck. The Band-Aid on Natalie Keene's knee. I could feel her name glowing hotly under my shirtsleeve.

This scene is mostly comprised of Camille's internal observations, but they are filled with sensory imagery—we feel the heat of blood rushing into her face, the sweat rising on her skin, and the thump of her heart, and it creates a momentum that keeps the pulse of the story racing forward instead of veering too much into the ether of her thoughts.

WEAVING THOUGHT AND SETTING IN FIRST PERSON

Another way to keep from slowing down the pace with character thoughts is to invoke visual setting details. Here's an example that weaves interior monologue with setting details in first person, from Nathan Filer's novel, *The Shock of the Fall*, about a boy who struggles with schizophrenia. Again, even though we are deep inside protagonist Matthew's thoughts, the scene provides enough physical detail to offer a concrete visual and sense of time that makes us feel the story moving forward:

> What happened next is less clear in my mind because it has merged into so many other memories, been played out in so many other ways that I can't separate the real from the imagined, or even be sure there is a difference. So I don't know exactly when she started to cry, or if she was crying already. And I don't know if she hesitated before throwing the last handful of dirt. But I do know by the time the doll was covered, and the earth patted

down, she was bent over, clutching the yellow coat to her chest, and weeping.

When you're a nine-year-old boy, it's no easy thing to comfort a girl. Especially if you don't know her, or even what the matter is.

I gave it my best show.

Intending to rest my arm lightly across her shoulders—the way Dad did to Mum when we took family walks—I shuffled forward, where in a moment of indecision I couldn't commit either to kneeling beside her or staying standing. I hovered awkwardly between the two, then overbalanced, toppling in slow motion, so the first this weeping girl was aware of me, was the entire weight of my body, gently pushing her face into a freshly dug grave.

First, the details of the girl crying and throwing a handful of dirt on a doll she is burying hold our attention while he sorts through the details of his memory, which could feel passive but don't. He then moves directly into physical actions that keep the pace moving forward.

First person is a wonderfully visceral, intimate POV that many readers enjoy. Writing it skillfully requires a careful blend of internal narration—thoughts, memories, observations—with active cues so that the plot never stagnates.

NOW YOU

SCOUR THE SURFACE

Pick a scene you're either struggling with or that you'd like to revise, or write one from scratch.

1. Identify your viewpoint character's surface feeling (one of the four main primary feelings).
2. Now, start combing through the scene for cues that point to other feelings. Make a list of the subset feelings these point to.

3. If you don't find enough cues, or you have too much exposition or narrative in place of cues, begin to add them. How can you convey the surface and subset emotions you're aiming for through dialogue, images, physical gestures, and so on? Try to come up with at least three cues to demonstrate character emotion in any given scene.

ACTIVE THOUGHTS

Write a scene in which your character makes several key internal observations, via his thoughts, about a situation that is causing him stress. Interweave this scene with physical action and/or setting details so that the forward momentum of your story doesn't slow. Here are a few examples:

- stumbling across an injured person
- meeting with a complicated person from the past
- visiting the scene of a crime

POETIC LICENSE

Write a poem from your protagonist's perspective, in which each line begins with the words "I am," and the answer to each line is a metaphor or a simile. For example: "I am a glass of cool water on a hot day" or "I am a moon waxing full." Let this poetic form allow you to draw on symbolic imagery that speaks to your character.

8

CLOSER AND CLOSER
Third-Person Intimate Point of View

> *"The trick to forgetting the big picture is to look at everything close up."*
>
> **—CHUCK PALAHNIUK**

Here's a secret about third-person intimate POV: It's just first-person POV wearing different clothes. Instead of the pronouns *I* and *me*, this viewpoint is clad in the pronouns *he/him* and *she/her*. Once you understand this essential difference, you will no longer mistake third-person intimate POV for omniscient POV merely because both use *he/she* pronouns.

But remember that POV is about much more than its pronouns; it is the camera, the lens and filter, through which your story is told. When you choose third-person intimate, you limit the amount of information you reveal to readers to only *one* character's eyes, mind, and heart per chapter or scene. By using *he/she* pronouns, however, you're offering slightly less intimacy between readers and the character.

I think third-person intimate is truly the most versatile POV. It provides intimacy and distance both; it prevents you from falling into the habit of sloppy head-jumping; and it forces you to hone your plot information, because you don't have the use of an omniscient narrator to toss information into the story whenever it's convenient.

SURFACE AND SUBSET EMOTIONS IN THIRD-PERSON INTIMATE

As with other points of view, it is surface and subset feelings that make characters so rich and rounded in third-person intimate. Let's look at some examples.

Jennifer McMahon's ghostly novel *The Winter People* follows Martin and Sara, a couple who live in a rural part of Vermont in the early 1900s. When their baby boy dies, Sara becomes emotionally frail, and as a result, when they have a second child, Gertie, she grows unnaturally bonded to her daughter, often refusing to let her out of her sight. On the advice of others, Martin tries to put distance between his wife and their daughter, which he ultimately regrets, after Gertie falls down a well to her death; maybe if he had let her stay close to her mother, she would be alive.

In the scene below, Martin believes Gertie's death has unhinged his wife from reality, and yet he's also worried about his own sanity. After hunting a fox and hanging the pelt, he later finds that the pelt is missing—and in its place is a lock of his daughter's hair. The surface feeling in the following scene is doubt: Martin doubts his wife's declaration that Gertie was murdered. But watch for cues that reveal deeper layers to Martin's feelings, and note how McMahon never tells the reader directly what he's feeling but instead demonstrates it through words, actions, and powerful visual and metaphoric imagery:

> She took in a sharp breath, held her head high. "I believe it is possible that Gertie did not fall down that well."

       Writing the Intimate Character

"But Sara, how do you explain—"

"I believe she may have been murdered."

Martin dropped his spoon, and it clattered to the floor.

"You cannot be serious," he said, once he'd regained his composure.

"Quite serious, Martin."

"And on what basis ..."

Sara smiled calmly. "Gertie told me," she said.

All the air left his chest, and the room suddenly got dim. Sara seemed far away and small. There she was, across the old pine table from him, an untouched bowl of stew before her. The oil lamp flickered at the center of the table; the fire in the old cast-iron cookstove crackled. The window above the kitchen sink was frost-covered, the night outside blacker than black. He couldn't even see a trace of stars.

Sara's face, pale as the moon, seemed to get smaller still. He reached out for her, his fingertips brushing the edge of the table.

It was as if he were falling, tumbling, spinning, down, down, all the way to the bottom of the well.

- **DIALOGUE CUES:** Martin's words ("How do you explain" and "You cannot be serious") convey his inner denial and doubt. We understand that he doesn't believe his wife's supposition that Gertie was murdered and that Gertie's ghost told his wife this information. His conclusion: His wife is insane. And yet, the subset cues reveal a deeper doubt as the scene continues.
- **PHYSICAL ACTION CUES:** Martin's actions suggest that some part of him thinks his wife might be right. The way he drops the spoon, which clatters to the floor, suggests an emotion that extends beyond doubt: fear, perhaps.
- **IMAGISTIC CUES:** Sara's face is described as "pale as the moon" and as growing smaller even though she hasn't moved farther away from Martin. These are symbolic images that cue the subset feelings of shock or fear. The night outside is "blacker than black," which conveys terror or despair.

- **SENSORY CUES:** It's in the sensory cues that readers begin to understand (and simultaneously feel in themselves) that one of Martin's subset feelings is not just doubt in his wife but horror or even terror. The sentence "All the air left his chest, and the room suddenly got very dim," contains sensations associated with shock and fear. McMahon then uses specific sensory details—the oil lamp flickering, the fire crackling, the window covered in frost—to create the sensation of time standing still. The description of Sara's face as "far away and small," and of Martin feeling as though he's looking at her from the bottom of the well where his daughter died, add up to something much more horrifying than doubt: *guilt*. Does Martin perhaps feel guilty? Readers—and Martin himself—begin to wonder: Is it possible that Martin murdered his own daughter?

Let's look at another excerpt, this time from Hanya Yanagihara's award-winning novel *A Little Life*. The "he" in this scene is the protagonist, Jude—a tortured character with a terrible secret history of abuse he has shared with no one, not even his closest friends or the people who have served as his mentors and parent figures. He was orphaned as a baby and raised by abusive monks and then suffered repeated sexual abuse after he was kidnapped from the monastery by one monk. In the following scene, his close friends Harold and Julia, older folks who have in many ways acted as his surrogate parents over the years, are preparing to ask if they can formally adopt him even though he is already thirty years old. To them, it's a symbolic act to make him officially a part of their family. However, Jude believes they've asked to speak with him to cut ties because he doesn't feel worthy of their love:

> He lowered himself to the sofa, and Harold to the chair to his left, and Julia to the squashed suzani-covered ottoman facing him: the places they always sat, the low table between them, and he wished the moment would hold itself, for what if this was the last one he would have here, the last time he would sit in this warm dark room, with its books and tart, sweet scent of cloudy apple

juice and the navy-and-scarlet Turkish carpet that had buckled itself into pleats under the coffee table, and the patch on the sofa cushion where the fabric had worn thin and he could see the white muslin skin beneath—all the things that he'd allowed to grow so dear to him, because they were Harold and Julia's, and because he had allowed himself to think of their house as his.

For a while they all sipped at their drinks, and none of them looked at the other, and he tried to pretend that this was just a normal evening, although if it had been a normal evening, none of them would be so silent.

"Well," Harold began at last, and he set his cup down on the table, readying himself. *Whatever he says*, he reminded himself, *don't start making excuses for yourself. Whatever he says, accept it, and thank him for everything.*

There was another long silence. "This is hard to say," Harold continued, and shifted his mug in his hand, and he made himself wait through Harold's next pause. "I really did have a script prepared, didn't I?" he asked Julia, and she nodded. "But I'm more nervous than I thought I would be."

"I know," she said. "But you're doing great."

"Ha!" Harold replied. "It's sweet of you to lie to me, though," and smiled at her, and he had the sense that it was only the two of them in the room, and that for a moment, they had forgotten he was there at all. But then Harold was quiet again, trying to say what he'd say next.

"Jude, I've—we've—known you for almost a decade now," Harold said at last, and he watched as Harold's eyes moved to him and then moved away, to somewhere above Julia's head. "And over those years, you've grown very dear to us; both of us. You're our friend, of course, but we think of you as more than a friend to us; as someone more special than that." He looked at Julia and she nodded at him once more. "So I hope you won't think this is too—presumptuous, I suppose—but we've been wondering if you might consider letting us, well, adopt you." Now he turned to him again, and smiled. "You'd be our legal son, and our legal heir, and someday all this"—he tossed his free arms into the air in a parodic gesture of expansiveness—"will be yours, if you want it."

He was silent. He couldn't speak; he couldn't react; he couldn't even feel his face, couldn't sense what his expression might be, and Julia hurried in. ... "Jude," she said, "if you don't want to, for whatever reason, we understand completely. It's a lot to ask. If you say no, it won't change how we feel about you, right, Harold? You'll always, always be welcome here, and we hope you'll always be part of our lives. Honestly, Jude—we won't be angry, and you shouldn't feel bad." She looked at him. "Do you want some time to think about it?"

And then he could feel the numbness receding, although as if in compensation, his hands began shaking, and he grabbed one of the throw pillows and wrapped his arms around it to hide them.

Later, when the conversation is over and Jude has accepted Harold and Julia's offer to adopt him, he reflects on the earth-shattering events that have just taken place:

> When he reached his room, he had to lie on the bed for half an hour before he could even think of retrieving his phone. He needed to feel the solidity of the bed beneath him, the silk of the cotton blanket against his cheek, the familiar yield of the mattress as he moved against it. He needed to assure himself that this was his world, and he was still in it, and what had happened had really happened.

Now let's look at the subset cues in this scene, which indicate what is happening within Jude:

- **PHYSICAL ACTION CUES:** All of Jude's physical actions speak to the surface feelings of anxiety and nervousness. His hands shake, and he clutches a pillow to his chest. He stares longingly at the items of Harold and Julia's house as though it will be the last time he ever sees them, suggesting a fear of impending loss.
- **DIALOGUE CUES:** Notice that Jude doesn't say anything during the scene; Harold and Julia provide the dialogue cues. Harold's halting, stuttering attempts to speak create a feeling of tension in

both readers and Jude, who is already poised to think the worst of any situation involving a loved one. At first, Harold's words, and the manner in which he delivers them, do nothing to dispel Jude's anxiety.

- **SENSORY CUES:** All of Jude's sensory cues are consistent with shock, trauma, and post-traumatic stress disorder. He alternates between numbness as he waits to hear Harold's reveal, and a kind of desperate clinging to the physical world, even after he hears the good news: "He needed to feel the solidity of the bed beneath him, the silk of the cotton blanket against his cheek, the familiar yield of the mattress as he moved against it." You can see how emotionally stunted Jude is; he may have a man's body, but he is essentially still an unloved child.

- **INTERNAL MONOLOGUE CUES:** Here, we see the real truth of Jude's subset feelings in his thoughts, and in the narrative voice: "*Whatever he says*, he reminded himself, *don't start making excuses for yourself. Whatever he says, accept it, and thank him for everything.*" Before Harold even extends the offer of adoption, Jude is coaching himself to be gracious; he assumes he will be sent away or asked to return his keys to their apartment. In his thoughts, and even in some of his words, Jude apologizes for his very existence. And even as the scene goes on, all he can imagine is the worst. It adds up to a subset feeling deeper than anxiety or fear—Jude feels *shame*. At his core, Jude is so wounded he can't imagine that he is worthy of this love, of being claimed by a family at long last. These kinds of complex emotions persist throughout the novel, even as Jude changes and heals in some ways. In strong characters, you'll often find several layers of subset feelings.

INTRODUCING CHARACTERS IN THIRD-PERSON INTIMATE

Earlier in the book we discussed internal and external proximity to your character. Third-person intimate may confuse the new writer because of the distance that *he* and *she* pronouns create. In third-person intimate, you're still *inside* your character's experience. That means you can't include external descriptions of your character unless it is conveyed through another character's eyes, with the use of a reflective surface such as a mirror, or in dialogue. That means your character will not notice her own "rosy cheeks" or "dazzling smile." However, you could write that she "felt the heat of embarrassment burning her face," and "the muscles in her cheeks strained to hold this false smile of cheer." The latter two phrases are internal descriptions of how the character feels. Notice, too, how these descriptions are far more effective because they avoid clichéd images and focus on emotions as well as physicality.

Of course, this character could also notice her rosy cheeks as she leans over a make-up counter at Macy's or passes a glass storefront. But in third-person intimate, you must take care to stick to the internal landscape of your character's experience for the majority of your descriptions. If you want to be able to offer external observations of a character, you should choose the omniscient POV or use the viewpoints of other characters to describe your character.

David Mitchell's genre-bending novel *Cloud Atlas* is a series of interlinked stories set in a multitude of time lines from the distant past to the imagined future. The author uses the descriptions of viewpoint characters to observe and comment on other key characters in the novel, which is a great way to introduce characters to readers in this POV.

In the following excerpt, we're introduced to two characters: Rufus Sixsmith, an aging physicist and soon-to-be whistle-blower on the devious doings of the Seaboard corporation's HYDRA project, and protagonist Luisa Rey, a lonely gossip-magazine writer with underutilized talents who is attending a party next door to Rufus's home. Mitchell uses each character's viewpoint to introduce the other in individual third-person intimate scenes—we see Luisa through Sixsmith's eyes and Sixsmith through Luisa's eyes. Mitchell also switches scenes between characters to signal to readers that he is moving into a new POV.

Rufus Sixsmith leans over the balcony and estimates his body's velocity when it hits the sidewalk and lays his dilemmas to rest. A telephone rings in the unlit room. Sixsmith dares not answer. Disco music booms from the next apartment, where a party is in full swing, and Sixsmith feels older than his sixty-six years. ...

A young woman emerges from the next-door party and leans over the neighboring balcony. Her hair is shorn, her violet dress is elegant, but she looks incurably sad and alone. *Propose a suicide pact, why don't you?* Sixsmith isn't serious, and he isn't going to jump either, not if an ember of humor still glows. *Besides, a quiet accident is precisely what Grimaldi, Napier, and those sharp-suited hoodlums are praying for.*

We do get a few details about Sixsmith, mostly about how he feels, though none of them are visual. We *are* told his age, which helps us begin to form a picture of him. However, it's not until we enter Luisa's POV, when the two characters meet and subsequently get stuck in an elevator together, that we are finally able to see Sixsmith through Luisa's eyes:

The elevator doors close just as Luisa Rey reaches them, but the unseen occupant jams them with his cane. "Thank you," says Luisa to the old man. "Glad the age of chivalry isn't totally dead."

He gives a grave nod.

Luisa thinks, *He looks like he's been given a week to live.* She presses G. The ancient elevator begins its descent. A leisurely needle counts off the stories. Its motor whines, its cables grind, but between the tenth and ninth stories a *gatta-gatta-gatta* detonates then dies with a *phzzz-zzz-zz-z.* Luis and Sixsmith thump to the floor. The light stutters on and off before settling on a buzzing sepia.

"You okay? Can you get up?"

The sprawled old man recovers himself a little. "No bones broken, I think, but I'll stay seated, thank you." His old-school English accent reminds Luisa of the tiger in *The Jungle Book.*

You don't always have to describe a character's physical features to show him to readers. In this passage, we come away with a strong impression that Sixsmith is elderly, frail, probably pale, gaunt, and dark-eyed, even though Luisa never once describes his features as such. It's phrases like "looks like he's been given a week to live" and the fact that he uses a cane and falls when the elevator stops that allow us to discern these details.

OBSERVING THE SETTING IN THIRD-PERSON INTIMATE

Third person-intimate creates a slight distance between readers and a character, but don't let yourself be tempted to write long expository passages of setting description. While your character's world may be of the utmost delight to *you*, remember the golden rule: Readers care about people first and places later. It's not that places aren't important—they absolutely are. Sometimes a particularly rich, vivid, wild setting is like a character itself; think of places like New Orleans or Paris. Yet you can communicate so many details about setting through action and dialogue without any need for lengthy expository passages.

In Chuck Wendig's science fiction novel *Under the Empyrean Sky,* the setting is an integral part of the characters' lives. They live in a dystopian world under "Empyrean" rule, amidst genetically modified, partially sentient corn that powers the world, and they rarely get to eat anything more than "shuck rats" and bland root vegetables. When protagonist Cael and his team of scavengers are out one day looking for whatever they can find to trade for "ace notes"—the currency in this world—they discover something that will change their fates and put them in terrible danger. Notice how the setting is shown mostly through the characters' interaction with it, in third-person intimate POV. Wendig rarely stops to engage in a long description of setting. Instead, he walks his characters into and through it.

> Cael sees another glimpse of the rat's tail and shoulders his way through the corn, chin to his chest, so as not to cut himself up further. He's got the slingshot in his hand, a ball bearing from

an old, broken-down motorvator pinched between thumb and forefinger in the pocket of the sling. His forearm is tensed.

The rat darts right, then left, zigzagging. Cael struggles to keep up. He sees a flash of gray—how'd the rat get over there?

One of the rats squeals—a sound that always cuts to Cael's marrow when he hears it, like fingers on a chalkboard but so much worse because it's coming up out of the throat of a howling, screaming mangy-ass rat—and bolts for the margin of the clearing. Cael's so stunned that he misses the shot, but the second rat isn't so lucky. Cael's brain catches up with his hand, and he opens his thumb and forefinger. The metal *thwacks* the rat in the head.

The rat gives him one last sad look before toppling over.

Cael laughs. Then he calls to his friends. Because they're going to want to see this.

The first thing that draws Cael's eyes are the red bell peppers, fat and swollen like breasts. They hang so low they're almost touching the ground. But soon his eyes move to see the bulging green beans, the jaunty onion tops, the round cabbage so richly purple it matches the iridescent back of a caviling grackle bird.

"Ohhhh" is all Rigo can say.

Lane is more verbose. "It's a garden. A glorious, no-shit, shouldn't-be-here, how-the-hell-can-it-survive garden."

Cael laughs, nudges the dead shuck rat aside with his foot, and grabs a red pepper. He twists it, and it pops off the plant. Then he takes a deep bite.

When you reveal setting through a character's interaction with it, the pace and tension remain tight and compelling. Any necessary details that you don't have time to communicate to readers in the narrative voice or description can be revealed in dialogue.

Here, we learn through Lane's dialogue that this garden is quite the anomaly, something that defies expectation simply by existing in the barren, poisoned landscape, and which poses a series of problems for the characters, as it's illegal to grow fruit or vegetables. All their food comes from the Empyrean. Later in the passage, as the boys eat some of this food that tastes fresher than anything they've ever eat-en, they discuss, in dialogue, what to do about their find. They can't tell anyone about it, or else they'll get in trouble with the government proctors. Wendig rarely slows down to explain anything about this world. Rather, he lets his characters' interactions with the setting slowly reveal crucial details.

WEAVING THOUGHTS AND ACTION IN THIRD-PERSON INTIMATE

In third-person intimate, because of the distance the *he/she* pronouns offer, you might find it easier to highlight the thoughts of a character in italics and intersperse them with the character's actions so that you don't create too much distance between reader and character, or slow down the pace too much. It's always better to create a balance of action and internal reflection—the less time you linger in thoughts, the better—but that doesn't mean you need to avoid them. Simply interweave them with the action.

Here's an example from Lidia Yuknavitch's *The Small Backs of Children*. In this scene, a character known as The Playwright has come to the hospital where his sister has fallen into a state of near-suicidal depression. He feels guilty for not visiting her more often, as he knows how much he means to her. Yuknavitch offers his thoughts in two ways: both in the narrative voice and in italics (which consist of lines of a play his sister once improvised):

> He opens his mouth and whisper-speaks to his sister between the pulses of the heart monitor. "Where are you?" He stares at their hands. Everything they are now is in their hands. He puts his head down. He kisses her hand once, twice, three times. The magic of fairy tales and children. She doesn't stir. People don't know anything about love. It's nothing, they told us. *Fate moves over the small backs of children. They carry death for us the second they are born.*
>
> He returns to the hallway, pacing in and out and in and out and in and out of the doorway. He sits back down.

Remember that if you are relying too heavily on internal monologue, this may be an indication that you are struggling with writing action in your scenes. If so, you need to find a way to shift the balance. Focus more on what your character does and says, and less on what he thinks.

NOW YOU

PHYSICAL FEATURE CHALLENGE

In third-person intimate, describe your viewpoint character without specifically describing her physical features. If she is tall, show her peering down at her friend "as though from a high ledge." If he has cropped, spiky hair, maybe "he ran his fingers through the cropped bristles of his new haircut, his scalp suddenly feeling too exposed to the elements." See how much you can convey indirectly.

A DASH THROUGH THE SETTING

Pick a setting in your story that plays a big part in your plot. Show us the setting using only your character's interactions with it. Steer clear of long-winded visual descriptions. Use each of your character's senses to realize one element of the world. You can also use dialogue.

9

IT'S A PARTY
Omniscient Point of View

*"It's easy to be omniscient
when you've done it all before."*

—AUDREY NIFFENEGGER, *THE TIME TRAVELER'S WIFE*

When you write in the omniscient point of view, your narrative voice
is like a superlibrarian who has access to all the answers, thoughts,
feelings, opinions, and events of the characters and the story. This
voice doles out information as needed. In omniscient, readers are not
seated the whole time in the up-close-and-personal internal viewpoint
of the protagonist. Instead, they are watching the protagonist's story
unfold in the theater of their own minds. In omniscient you can move
from a highly external and distant perspective in one paragraph to

a close, internal perspective in the next, so long as the switch makes sense to the story and isn't too jarring for readers.

Omniscient also allows you to pull knowledge from historical contexts that exist outside the parameters of the story's time period—either in the past or the future—and also move to other locations and other characters' heads without changing scenes.

This POV is both incredibly versatile and quite difficult to manage if you haven't yet mastered it. Omniscient allows you to move between internal and external viewpoints as needed, hop into the heads of multiple characters in a single scene, and offer information above, beyond, and outside the scope of the protagonist's direct experience through an "all-knowing" narrator. These challenges present multiple opportunities for confusion and sloppy storytelling.

Along with examples of character cues in omniscient, we will explore the errors that writers can make when using this POV so you can avoid them in your own fiction.

INTRODUCING CHARACTERS IN OMNISCIENT

If you're the kind of writer who enjoys describing your character's personality or physical features in ways he would not think to describe himself, and if you like to provide intel about your character that isn't always filtered through actions and dialogue, the omniscient POV allows you the greatest latitude. In omniscient you truly are a god or goddess. Just make sure you are a benevolent supreme being who doesn't jerk readers in too many directions. (We'll talk more on that issue later in this chapter.)

Here are a few different examples of how to handle character introductions in omniscient. First, let's look at Donna Tartt's *The Little Friend*, a sprawling novel that straddles the literary and mystery genres:

> Harriet had none of her sister's dreamy fragility. She was sturdily built, like a small badger, with round cheeks, a sharp nose, black hair bobbed short, a thin, determined little mouth. She spoke

briskly, in a reedy, high-pitched voice that for a Mississippi child was oddly clipped, so that strangers often asked where on earth she had picked up that Yankee accent. Her gaze was pale, penetrating, and not unlike Edie's. The resemblance between her and her grandmother was pointed, and did not go unremarked; but the grandmother's quick, fierce-eyed beauty was in the grandchild merely fierce, and a trifle unsettling.

The following clues tell us that this scene is in omniscient:

- **FREE-FLOATING OBSERVATIONS:** The opinions and observations about Harriet are delivered externally, as though from someone else: This narrator has formed an opinion that Harriet's accent is "oddly clipped," that the resemblance between her and her grandmother is "pointed," and that her beauty is "a trifle unsettling."
- **NOT SPECIFIC TO THE CHARACTER:** These descriptions are not Harriet's opinions—she would not think of herself in this way.
- **JUST THE FACTS:** Information is delivered about Harriet as though the narrator is giving a report on her. The details are not filtered through Harriet's own experience—instead they come from an external vantage point.

In the following excerpt from Gina Frangello's *A Life in Men*, the two main characters are introduced in omniscient. In the first two lines, the narrator appears to be a ghost of the already-dead character Nix, speaking in the first-person (reminiscent of Alice Sebold's *The Lovely Bones*), but then quickly drops into an omniscient voice that not only knows details about both girls that are not filtered through their POVs, but also knows details about the future:

Pretend I'm not already dead. That isn't important anyway. It's just that from here, I can see everything.

There we are, see? Or should I say, *There they are*? Two girls sitting at a café off Taxi Square, eating anchovies lined up in a small puddle of oil on a white plate. Both girls are obsessed with salt. … The curly-haired blonde girl, Mary, jokes to the straight-haired blonde girl, Nix, that this influx of salt is going to be a turnoff should they pick up on any hot men. Mary has cystic fibrosis, and sometimes one of the first clues parents get that their baby has CF is that the child's sweat is especially salty. …

Meanwhile, the imaginary camera, abetted by the very real script, has established that Nix is the wilder of the two. What of it, though? Her weakly blinking pride in this fact is perpetually diminished by the chronic illness of the other, so that ordinary acts like going to Greece for two weeks before the start of their junior year of college take on—for Mary—a kind of heroism that all Nix's wild antics pale beside, as she is not sick, just nineteen and reckless and normal, with all the luxurious frustrations normalcy affords. In two weeks, Mary will return home to her parents' house in Kettering, Ohio, whereas Nix will spend the first semester of her junior year at Regent's College in London.

So what are the clues that tell us we're in omniscience?

- **EXTERNAL DESCRIPTIONS:** The pronoun *they* is used when describing Mary and Nix from the external POV. Yet there is no other character in the scene through whose eyes we could be looking, so we are clearly in omniscient.
- **THE NARRATIVE VOICE TELLS US DIRECTLY:** The sentence "Meanwhile the imaginary camera, abetted by the very real script, has established that Nix is the wilder of the two," is delivered from an external viewpoint. It isn't internally within Nix's perspective but is looking in from the outside. Other phrases describe the girls externally: "weakly blinking pride" and "reckless and normal."
- **INFORMATION IS NOT REVEALED BY CHARACTERS:** The reader learns information about cystic fibrosis that isn't offered by one of the characters.
- **TIME TRAVEL:** The narrator knows the future of these girls: "In two weeks, Mary will return home to her parents' house in Kettering, Ohio, whereas Nix will spend the first semester of her junior year at Regent's College in London."

MOVING FROM ONE CHARACTER'S HEAD TO ANOTHER'S

The omniscient viewpoint is most commonly used in two ways: (1) as an all-knowing external narrator, and (2) as a series of "roving heads." In the latter method, omniscience allows you to move between the POVs of different characters without having to stop the scene and start a new one, as in the intimate POVs. This is fantastic when you don't want to stop the action to get into another character's head. But it can also be confusing for readers if you spend considerable time in one character's head and establish what appears to be a limited viewpoint, only to suddenly jump into another character's head.

For example, here's a scene from a hypothetical novel in which two sisters are trying to help their youngest sister, who has just decided on the eve of her wedding that she wants to call it off. We'll call the sisters Alice, Beverly, and Claire. Claire, the youngest, is the protagonist. However, her sisters appear in many scenes with her, so they're "onscreen" a lot, too, which is common with important secondary characters.

Here's an example of how you might confuse a reader by switching too quickly between the POVs of the sisters:

> Claire put her head between her knees, her breath trapped there, whether due to the heavy wool fabric of her skirt or the pressure of dread at tomorrow's wedding. Alice had to force down a frustrated sigh. Leave it to Claire, the baby, to be so wishy-washy at the last minute about something as major as marriage, as though the world should just bow to her every whim. Beverly, too, was biting her tongue, but not because she judged Claire's choice to call off the wedding; she wished she'd had her sister's strength a decade ago, before she got so deeply into her own imperfect union.

When you shift between characters' thoughts, you leave more room for blurring and blending between characters in confusing ways. A more effective way to transition between the sisters would be to give each one a physical gesture or line of dialogue that announces a transition from one to the next.

Here's the revised version:

> Alice sighed and smoothed the folds of her skirt. "Claire, darling, just because you're used to getting your every whim fulfilled does not make this a good idea. Months of planning have gone into this. You know he'll never speak to you again," she said.
>
> Claire only sobbed harder at this.
>
> Beverly, too, was biting her tongue, but not because she judged Claire's choice to call off the wedding. "Well I disagree, Alice. I wish I'd had Claire's strength a decade ago, before I flounced blithely into my own imperfect union."
>
> Alice shook her head. "This isn't strength; it's cowardice."
>
> Claire sat up so fast she saw stars. "Stop talking about me like I'm not here!"

USING OMNISCIENT TO PROVIDE INFORMATION CHARACTERS CANNOT KNOW

In some novels there comes a time when you need to deliver information to the reader that the character can't offer herself, either because she doesn't yet know it or because it has or will happen outside the time frame of the story.

Michael Cunningham's literary novel *The Hours* follows the stories of three characters in three different decades, including a fictional version of the author Virginia Woolf, who committed suicide in real life in 1941. Early in the novel, Cunningham describes the scene of Woolf's death from an omniscient point of view. As morbid as it may seem, it is an important and emotionally laden scene that serves to make later scenes of Woolf—which flash back to when she was alive—even more vivid and palpable.

> She is borne quickly along by the current. She appears to be flying, a fantastic figure, arms outstretched, hair streaming, the tail of the fur coat billowing behind. She floats, heavily, through shafts of brown, granular light. She does not travel far. Her feet (the

shoes are gone) strike the bottom occasionally, and when they do they summon up a sluggish cloud of muck, filled with the black silhouettes of leaf skeletons, that stands all but stationary in the water after she has passed along out of sight. ...

A small boy, no older than three, crossing the bridge with his mother, stops at the rail, crouches, and pushes the stick he's been carrying between the slats of the railing so it will fall into the water. His mother urges him along but he insists on staying awhile, watching the stick as the current takes it.

Here they are, on a day early in the Second World War: the boy and his mother on the bridge, the stick floating over the water's surface, and Virginia's body at the river's bottom, as if she is dreaming of the surface, the stick, the boy and his mother, the sky and the rooks.

In this scene Virginia is dead, so we are not getting her experience or POV. Likewise, no one is watching her body floating down the river until the end of the scene, when a little boy sees her body. Even then, the language of the descriptions is too mature to be in his POV. It is simply omniscient information, given to us in the narrative voice because the author feels it is important. And it certainly sets a mood, a tone of somberness and tragedy that capped Virginia Woolf's life. It also allows us into a moment that real life didn't allow. The author takes artistic license that results in a passage both lyrical and sad.

USING OMNISCIENCE TO PROVIDE A PAUSE

Sometimes the intensity of a scene requires a moment of pause, of pulling back and away, which acts like a palate cleanser for readers. In this space between two intense moments, the omniscient POV can be used to zoom the reader away from an intimate internal viewpoint to a removed external position.

In Gina Frangello's *A Life in Men*, college girls Mary and Nix have spent the past forty-eight hours trapped in the villa of two Greek men they went home with. Fearing for their lives, Nix makes a deal to protect Mary, who suffers from cystic fibrosis: She offers herself to the men, but what happens to her is more violent than she anticipated. Mary does not know what happened to Nix, only that it bought them their freedom. There is a strange tension between the two of them afterwards. Frangello, who primarily uses third-person intimate POV in the novel, now pulls back into the omniscient, which allows readers to remove themselves temporarily from the emotional intensity but also readies them for the intense scenes that follow:

> Note how out of place they are among the other passengers: locals commuting for business, or families—tourist and Greek—with young children. Other backpackers of their ilk are all still in rented rooms rendered dark by drawn curtains, sleeping off the island merriments of the night before. Wordlessly the girls find a bench in the sun, in their exhaustion mistaking the air for chilly, though already the sun beats down relentless. If they were thinking straight, they would find seats inside, away from the glare, but instead they sit on a white painted bench out in the open, jean jackets clutched around their shoulders, hair piled up in disheveled knots atop their heads, rucksacks on the bench between them so as to have something on which to lean or a barrier to deter each other from sitting too close. The ferry sets off into rocky waves, and still the two are silent.

We know we are in the omniscient in this scene by the use of the pronoun *they*, which lumps the POVs of both girls into one. In an intimate, limited POV, you can deliver only one character's perspective and thoughts at a time. Also, the phrase "so as to have something on which to lean or a barrier to deter each other from sitting too close" is not delivered by either girl but by the all-knowing narrator who offers a separate assumption that doesn't come from the characters.

USING OMNISCIENT TO PROVIDE HISTORICAL CONTEXT

Historical novels, or novels in a series, often need to provide historical context so readers will know the time period or certain historical data that would take too much time to reveal through character dialogue or action. In these cases, omniscience is necessary to provide this information. Take this example from J.K. Rowling's *Harry Potter and the Goblet of Fire*:

> The villagers of Little Hangleton still called it "the Riddle House," even though it had been many years since the Riddle family had lived there. It stood on a hill overlooking the village, some of its windows boarded, tiles missing from its roof, and ivy spreading unchecked over its face. Once a fine-looking manor, and easily the largest and grandest building for miles around, the Riddle House was now damp, derelict, and unoccupied.
>
> The Little Hangletons all agreed that the old house was "creepy." Half a century ago, something strange and horrible had happened there, something that the older inhabitants of the village still liked to discuss when topics for gossip were scarce. The story had been picked over so many times, and had been embroidered in so many places, that nobody was quite sure what the truth was anymore.

Rowling uses the omniscient POV to reveal information about the spooky Riddle house, which plays an important role in major plot revelations later in the story, and in the series overall. The information isn't revealed through any character's POV; it's the all-knowing librarian at work, telling us what we need to know in order to delve deeper into the story.

Just remember that more than a few paragraphs of this type of characterless perspective will eventually slacken the pace. Make sure to intersperse historical context alongside action and dialogue.

Writing the Intimate Character

SURFACE AND SUBSET FEELING CUES IN OMNISCIENT

The omniscient POV provides cues to what the characters are feeling and thinking in a different way than more intimate POVs. Some of the cues will be the same, but omniscient also allows for more shortcuts, as the narrator can simply tell the reader what the character thinks or feels. In other words, due to the fluidity of the POV, the subset emotions may actually be more evident than in other POVs.

Here's a passage from the multigenerational family saga *Fall on Your Knees* by Ann-Marie MacDonald. I've included italicized notes in brackets to point out the cues and other points of interest:

> [James] had already removed a few ivory keys and was bent under the lid behind the piano's gap-toothed smile, so he didn't see Materia when she stepped into the archway. [*Omniscient POV allows for the narrator to reveal things the character can't see. Here, James didn't see Materia, but we see them both.*]
>
> But she had seen him. She had spied him from her upstairs bedroom window when he came knocking at the kitchen door below, toting his earnest bag of tools—a blond boy so carefully combed. She had peeked at him through the mahogany railings carved with grapes as he entered the front hall and hung his coat in the closet beneath the stairs—his eyes so blue, his skin so fair. [*Her descriptions of him may seem benign, but they are loaded with yearning. His eyes are "so" blue and his skin is "so" fair—qualifications that suggest she admires these features.*] Taut and trim, collar, tie and cufflinks. Like a China figurine. Imagine touching his hair. Imagine if he blushed. [*Why imagine "if he blushed" unless it's something she'd like to see?*] She watched him cross the hall ... she followed him. [*Following him suggests she wants to know more.*]
>
> She paused in the archway, her weight on one foot, and considered him a moment. Thought of plucking his suspenders. Grinned to herself, crept over to the piano and hit C sharp. He sprang back with a cry—immediately Materia feared she'd gone too far, he must be really hurt, he's going to be really mad, she

bit her lip—he clapped a hand over one eye and beheld the culprit with the other.

The darkest eyes he'd ever seen, wet with light. [*In the omniscient you can jump suddenly into the mind of another character. Here, we've left Materia's POV and enters James's.*] Coal-black curls escaping from two long braids. Summer skin the color of sand stroked by the tide … [*The choice of description "stroked by the tide" suggests appreciation, desire.*] His right eye wept while his left eye rejoiced. [*This description of his eyes is external, from the omniscient narrator rather than inside the character.*] His lips parted silently. He wanted to say, "I know you," but none of the facts of his life backed this up so he merely stared, smitten and unsurprised.

She smiled and said, "I'm going to marry a dentist."

She had an accent that she never did outgrow. [*Here we've time traveled into the future just briefly, which you can only do in omniscient.*] A softening of consonants, a slightly liquid "r," a tendency to clip not with the lips but with the throat itself …

"I'm not a dentist," he said, then rushed pink to his ears.

She smiled.

Everything about the interactions between these characters, no matter whose mind we are actually in, adds up to attraction, flirtation, and desire, even though Materia's actions with the piano keys could be seen as aggressive or hostile.

CHARACTER INTERACTIONS WITH SETTING

In the intimate viewpoints, when you show your characters interacting with the setting, you will also often give cues as to their inner feelings about, and observations of, the setting. In the omniscient POV, you may show the character moving through the setting in an external way, without entering the inner landscape of the character.

Here's an example from Ingrid Hill's *Ursula, Under*:

A silhouette of indeterminate gender, dressed in a raggedy wool cape almost to the ground, appears in one of the castle's minor courtyards, climbing down from a tradesman's carriage. ...

The figure tugs hard at the bellpull. The white-capped head of a kitchen maid appears in a window just above.

"Yes?" she calls down.

"Cheeses from Holland!" announces the figure. "Brown rind and red rind. All excellent."

"What did you say? Did you say cheeses?" the maid calls.

The caped figure seems to reconsider.

"They have come from the far Azores," says the figure, a clearly feigned harshness. "If you do not hurry your insolent buttocks down here they will wilt, or freeze, and we will have yet one more international incident on our hands. Hurry!"

The maid closes the shutters and turns to consider. *My insolent buttocks*, she thinks, for she has indeed heard the second series of remarks, as the wind shifted. She laughs.

The scene begins from a great distance, and the viewpoint is quite removed from any character. The all-knowing eye of the omniscient narrator shows us a "silhouette of indeterminate gender," but we're not looking through any character's eyes until the maid enters the scene. Then, briefly, the opinions and observations become hers once the figure insults her. We enter her POV with the sentence, "The maid closes the shutters and turns to consider." In the next sentence we hear her thoughts: "*My insolent buttocks. ...*" The scene and the setting have temporarily become more intimate while we stay in her perspective. Later in the scene the POV jumps into external passages again, and into the heads of other characters.

You can see how fine the balance is when moving between characters' heads in omniscient. Sometimes pulling back to focus on the setting is a good way to segue or transition between characters without jarring the reader.

HABITS TO AVOID IN OMNISCIENCE

If you do choose to write in omniscient, stay vigilant against the following habits that lead to sloppy writing and may confuse your readers:

- **HEAD JUMPING TOO QUICKLY:** Many writers choose omniscience for the ability to move in and out of the minds of multiple characters throughout the course of the book. But try to avoid jumping from mind to mind too quickly or too often. Each scene should still have a goal for your protagonist—and readers are most interested in your protagonist. Devote a few paragraphs to a character before you leap and leap again.

- **HEAD JUMPING TOO SLOWLY:** On the other hand, in order to signal to the reader that you're in omniscient, particularly of the roving-heads variety, you don't want to go too many pages without establishing that you will be taking that liberty. Ideally, you should move into another character's POV within the first few pages and then jump back to your protagonist. If you wait dozens of pages to switch heads, the jump will seem like an accident.

- **STAYING TOO DISTANT OR EXTERNAL:** Since omniscience allows you to stay at a distance from your characters, it's easy to forget the need to zoom back in and get inside your character, too. Otherwise, the entire book could end up feeling like a long lecture about your character rather than a page-turning adventure alongside him.

- **AUTHORIAL INTRUSION:** Save your "dear reader" lines for your journal; when you offer information that comes from the "all-knowing" narrator, make sure it is still coming from within the story—and not from you directly.

At its worst, omniscience lends itself to sloppy storytelling habits like jumping too quickly or too often from character to character and confusing readers, or not quickly enough and slowing down the pace with overly long passages of history, setting description, or backstory. But it's also incredibly versatile. Remember that omniscience gives you room to move from the distant to the intimate and vice versa. It allows you to travel through time, to jump between characters' minds, and to call upon information outside the context of the individual scene.

NOW YOU

ZOOM THE LENS

Write a new scene. Start out in the distant, all-knowing omniscient POV, describing your character externally: how he looks, what he's doing. Then, within a paragraph or two, zoom internally so that suddenly we are inside your character and can hear, feel, and sense the scene from his perspective. Alternately, start the scene up close and then zoom out, pulling away from the intensity and intimacy.

FLASH FORWARD

Pick a scene in which the all-knowing narrator knows something about the future that your protagonist doesn't know and makes a future-tense leap to tell the reader a piece of information that hasn't yet been revealed. See if you can manage to give only a partial reveal of a plot detail and not the whole story.

10

ALL ABOUT *YOU*
Second-Person Point of View

> *"What people in the world think of you is really none of your business."*

—**MARTHA GRAHAM**

"You talkin' to me?" says a young Robert De Niro to his reflection in the mirror, playing the role of loner Travis Bickle in the film *Taxi Driver*. He is talking to himself, literally, in the mirror, but he is also talking to an imagined person he will confront later in the film. This scene reflects the variety of ways the second-person POV can be used in your fiction. Most commonly this POV is used as an even more intimate alternative to first person. It bypasses the conceit that the character is narrating to an audience—instead, the audience *is* the character.

DIFFERENT VERSIONS OF SECOND PERSON

Second-person POV can be used in a story in several ways. In the version of second-person POV used in the scene from *Taxi Driver, you* is self-talk—the character talking to himself. You rarely find an entire novel written in this form of the second person; *Bright Lights, Big City* by Jay McInerney is a noteworthy exception. While at one time I would have advised against using second person at all in fiction, I now find that literature continually pushes experimental boundaries. If you can employ it well in a manuscript, second person creates a wry, strange, but also interesting voice.

Otherwise, it's common to use second person to achieve certain effects within a story, for a variety of different reasons. In another variation of second person, the character talks directly to the audience, "Dear Reader" style, breaking the silent accord between reader and author and allowing the reader to eavesdrop on the story. In yet another variation, the narrator talks to a specific person who is not the audience. In this chapter, we'll look at the ways second person can be used to enhance your novel.

Second-Person Intimate: *You* As Self-Talk

If good fiction shows rather than tells, then second-person intimate is the ultimate tool for showing. It removes the veil between reader and character altogether, and it pushes past thoughts of the self with the pronoun *I*, invoking instead the way we talk or think to ourselves as we go about our daily lives. But as an avid reader who has come across this POV from time to time, I've observed that it is most commonly used to tell stories in which a character behaves badly or shamefully, or when the reader might perceive bad behavior.

Take the protagonist in Jay McInerney's *Bright Lights, Big City.* The novel opens without any real preamble; it starts with an unnamed man narrating his own debauchery. He's on the search for more "Bolivian

Marching Powder," a.k.a. cocaine, and he's firmly aware of his own bad behavior:

> All might come clear if you could just slip into the bathroom and do a little more Bolivian Marching Powder. Then again, it might not. A small voice inside you insists that this epidemic lack of clarity is a result of too much of that already. The night has already turned on that imperceptible pivot where two A.M. changes to six A.M. You know this moment has come and gone, but you are not yet willing to concede that you have crossed the line beyond which all is gratuitous damage and the palsy of unraveled nerve endings.

If this passage were written in first person, readers might easily judge the character for seeking illicit substances in the wee hours of the morning. Instead, via the miracle of second person, they can magically *become* the character, slip into his skin, and go along for the ride more willingly, while he carries on with abandon. As the scene continues, he ditches a woman at a nightclub to whom he refers as "the bald girl" and spots another woman whom he thinks "looks like your last chance for earthly salvation"—in other words, he views hooking up with this woman as justification for his bad behavior. The two do connect over a shared pleasure but not in the way he hopes:

> "You've got some blow?" she says.
>
> "Is Stevie Wonder blind?" you say.
>
> She takes your arm and leads you into the Ladies'. A couple of spoons and she seems to like you just fine, and you are feeling very likable yourself. A couple more. This woman is all nose.
>
> "I love drugs," she says, as you march toward the bar.
>
> "It's something we have in common," you say.
>
> "Have you ever noticed how all the good words start with D? D and L."
>
> You try to think about this. You're not quite sure what she's driving at. The Bolivians are singing their marching song, but you can't make out the words.
>
> "You know. Drugs. Delight. Decadence."

"Debauchery," you say, catching the tune now.

"Dexedrine."

"Delectable. Deranged. Debilitated."

"Delinquent."

"Delirium."

"And L," she says. "Lush and luscious."

"Languorous."

"Librium."

"Libidinous."

"What's that?" she says.

"Horny."

"Oh," she says, casting a long, arching look over your shoulder.

His "earthly salvation" ditches him once she realizes what he really wants. But rather than view him with the judgmental vision of an observer, we have, instead, *become* him, and thus feel for him.

In stories that feature an antihero, a protagonist with a long journey toward redemption, or a character who engages in questionable behavior, second person may offer a kind of freedom for readers to "participate" in a narrative that involves behavior they might not agree with. In other words, you're helping readers suspend their disbelief or judgment. Though most of this book focuses on fiction for the obvious reason that most memoir and nonfiction is written in first person, it's worth noting that writer Rob Roberge recently published a memoir called *Liar* in the second person, a very unusual stylistic choice, perhaps because even he needed just a little distance from his own story.

Plus, the protagonist of *Bright Lights, Big City* is not just a bad guy—he's a guy medicating away deep emotional pain, which is revealed over the course of the novel. He becomes more and more sympathetic as the roots of his behavior are revealed.

In another example, this version of second person offers an intimacy thematically linked to the subject matter. In Lorrie Moore's short story "How to be an Other Woman," the narrator is just that—a mistress—and the second person invites us to be the mistress with her.

When you were six you thought *mistress* meant to put your shoes on the wrong feet. Now you are older and know it can mean many things, but essentially it means to put your shoes on the wrong feet.

You walk differently. In store windows you don't recognize yourself; you are another woman, some crazy interior display lady in glasses stumbling frantic and preoccupied through the mannequins. In public restrooms you sit dangerously flat against the toilet seat, a strange flesh sundae of despair and exhilaration, murmuring into your bluing thighs: "Hello, I'm Charlene. I'm a mistress."

It is like having a book out from the library.

It is like constantly having a book out from the library.

What I like so much about the way Moore constructs this story is that she shows the unglamorous side of being a mistress. This is no *Fifty Shades of Grey* fantasy—it's suggestive of real life, both messy and complicated. She shows that being a mistress can also be dull and anxiety-ridden, not necessarily all romance and desire. And even when she does provide a glimpse of the physical intimacy with her lover, it's tinged with sadness:

Whisper, "Don't go yet," as he glides out of your bed before sunrise and you lie there on your back cooling, naked between the sheets and smelling of musky, oniony sweat. Feel gray, like an abandoned locker room towel. Watch him as he again pulls on his pants, his sweater, his socks and shoes. … In the smoky darkness, you see him smile weakly, guiltily, and attempt a false, jaunty wave from the doorway. Turn on your side, toward the wall, so you don't have to watch the door close.

Both *Bright Lights, Big City* and "How to be an Other Woman" offer us a way to imagine ourselves in the character's situation without having to surmount a barrier that obscures the character. It's difficult to read a novel when you're busy judging the character, but when you've slipped into the costume, the skin and brain of the protagonist, bad behaviors seem more the result of human frailty than of stupidity. It can be a brilliant device when used properly.

It can also, however, be a clunky and awkward device when not used well. It can lend itself to too much narrative reflection and slow down the pace. I find that the writers who wield it best have strong style and narrative voice—their very sentences and imagery are interesting, which aids the story's flow.

"As Told To" Second Person: *You* That Addresses Another Character

Plenty of writing guides will tell you it's no longer the convention to talk directly to the reader (particularly in the old "Dear Reader" style of the late seventeenth century), but some contemporary novels do contain a second-person POV in which the narrating protagonist talks directly to someone. In these instances, the whole book is a conversation with another character; is written as a letter or a story told in one long novel-length passage; or, as in Caroline Kepnes's novel, *You*, addresses a character from afar. In *You*, Joe is a youngish man who works at a New York City bookstore. When lovely young Beck comes in one day, Joe forms an unhealthy obsession with her. The entire novel is narrated from his POV in the second person, addressing Beck:

> Am I just another *stranger*? Is your Twitter bio your subtle way of announcing that you're an attention whore who has no standards and will give audience to any poor schmuck who says hello? Was I nothing to you? You don't even mention the guy in the bookstore? … Maybe we had nothing. But then I started to explore you and you don't write about what really matters. You wouldn't share me with your followers. Your online life is a variety show, so if anything, the fact that you didn't put me in your stand-up act means that you covet me. Maybe even more than I realize …

Joe is directing not only his active dialogue to Beck in this scene but also his internal musings and observations, as though he is composing a journal or a long letter to her. This is evident because he does occasionally refer to himself as "I," which lets us know that when he says "you" he means Beck, not himself.

Second Person Universal: *You* As Humanity

Perhaps the most common way to use second person is not as the POV for an entire novel but selectively, in passages or asides in which the narrator slips into universal language to convey a feeling, a mood, a concept, or a theme.

Haruki Murukami's novel *Kafka on the Shore* is mostly written in the first-person POV of the protagonist, a boy named Kafka. But in the following passage, in the midst of a conversation with a boy named Crow, Kafka slips into a second-person aside, which I've marked in bold:

> "Okay, picture a terrible sandstorm," he says. "Get everything else out of your head."
>
> I do what he says, get everything else out of my head. I forget who I am, even. I'm a total blank. Then things start to surface. Things that—as we sit here on the old leather sofa in my father's study—both of us can see.
>
> "Sometimes fate is like a small sandstorm that keeps changing directions," Crow says.
>
> Sometimes fate is like a small sandstorm that keeps changing directions. **You change direction but the sandstorm chases you. You turn again, but the storm adjusts. Over and over you play this out, like some ominous dance with death just before dawn. Why? Because this storm isn't something that blew in from far away, something that has nothing to do with you. This storm is you. Something *inside* of you. So all you can do is give in to it, step right inside the storm, closing your eyes and plugging up your ears so the sand doesn't get in, and walk through it, step by step.**

Let's examine this passage critically. Why does the author bother with the second person? Why couldn't he stay in first person, directly in

Kafka's POV? Murukami could, of course, but notice how the shift into the second person takes us deeper into metaphorical territory. It pushes not only the character but the reader to consider the philosophical questions at the heart of this paragraph. It once again merges reader with character and provokes emotional depth. In other words, it creates a tone, a mood of introspection that is an important part of this highly philosophical novel.

But even in more straightforward novels, the use of the second person universal is a way of discussing a concept, or evoking an idea, that brings in a larger context. It pulls an idea from the realm of the personal to explore human nature, making us think beyond our small selves.

Here's another example, from Marlon James's Man Booker Award–winning novel *A Brief History of Seven Killings*. (I need to give a content warning here before you proceed: This passage deals with rape.) We enter the scene with Nina Burgess, who finds herself in a terrifying situation in which she believes that she is about to be raped. She lives in Jamaica, in a town where victims are often blamed when they are raped, and where women feel powerless.

> You can't really know how it feels, just knowing deep down that in a few minutes these men will rape you. God take you make fool, this Cassandra from Greek mythology in history class who nobody listens to, who can't even hear herself. The men haven't touched you yet but you've already blamed yourself, you stupid naïve little bitch this is how man in uniform rape a woman, when you still think they are there to take your cat out of a tree, like this is a Dick and Dora story. … It's the slowness that gets you, the feeling that there is still time to do something, to get out, to run, to close your eyes and think of Treasure Beach. You have all the time in the world. Because when this happens it's your fault …

Here, the second-person POV serves two functions:

1. It unites Nina in a universal way with all women who have found themselves in such a powerless situation—she is speaking from more than just her own experience. Her use of the Greek Cassandra myth

further proves this, as Cassandra stands as a metaphor for the struggle of women: She was also powerless, raped by a god, and then given the "gift" to know the future and the curse of never being believed.

2. It puts some distance between reader and character. I like to think that James does this intentionally so that we will not stop reading—he provides a little distance so we can digest the coming terror.

Once we've been pulled into the passage, Nina drops back into first person, because by now we are invested in what happens to her:

> I heard a story about a woman who went to the police to report a rape but they didn't believe her so they raped her again.

In summary, use the second-person universal POV to convey universal or big-picture ideas or philosophies, provide momentary distance in an intense first-person experience, set a specific tone or a mood, or create extreme intimacy with your protagonist.

POTENTIAL PITFALLS FOR USING SECOND PERSON

It's easy to get a little sidetracked when writing second person. Its unorthodox form can cause you to wander off into tangents and asides, and it can create a kind of silliness or levity that may not always lend itself to the intensity of the scene you've written. It may not be the best POV for a socially gregarious character who is, by her nature, more external than internal. But it is wonderful for opening up the inner world of a shy, introspective, quirky, or highly intellectual character.

Avoid these pitfalls when writing in the second person:

- Don't forget to do the work of writing scenes. You must not forget to use action, dialogue, sensory imagery, and the many other cues we've discussed to keep the energy of a scene alive.
- Don't wander off into overly long internal monologue passages, which will slow the pace.

- Stick to the action. Focus on what your character does next to avoid the ethereal, time-dragging space of rumination.

SURFACE AND SUBSET EMOTIONS IN SECOND PERSON

Despite its unorthodox format, surface and subset emotions are still crucial in the second-person POV. In the following passage from *Bright Lights, Big City*, the narrator has made a huge error in proofreading a story that went into the magazine where he works, a mistake which has caused massive problems:

> From the window to Clara's office is a very short distance. Much too short. You are there. She slams the door from the inside, takes the seat in front of the desk and stares you down. She doesn't ask you to sit, so you do. This is shaping up even worse than you anticipated. ... You wish that you had paid more attention when a woman you met at Heartbreak told you about Zen meditation. Think of all this as an illusion. She can't hurt you. ...
>
> "I would like to know what happened."
>
> A dumb question. Far too general. You draw a good breath. "I screwed up." You might add that the writer of the piece in question really screwed up, that you improved the thing immeasurably, and that the change of scheduling was ill-advised. But you don't.
>
> "You screwed up."
>
> You nod. It's true. In this case, however, honesty doesn't make you feel a whole lot better. You're having trouble meeting her glare.
>
> "Just how did you screw up, exactly?"
>
> You're already gone. You are out the window with the pigeons. You try to alleviate the terror by thinking how ridiculous her French braids look, like spinnakers on a tugboat. You suspect that deep down she enjoys this.

- **PHYSICAL ACTION CUES:** He finds the walk to his boss's office "much too short"—meaning some part of him would like it to be longer. This suggests anxiety and fear.
- **SENSORY CUES:** There aren't many sensory cues in this passage, though his "having trouble meeting her glare" tells us something: He can't stand to look at her.
- **DIALOGUE CUES:** The narrator does not try to stall; he knows he can only come clean. So he confesses his wrongdoing: "I screwed up."
- **INTERNAL MONOLOGUE CUES:** He chides himself for not studying Zen meditation, as he thinks he could use the techniques now, and also castigates the "writer of the piece," whose bad writing, he feels, got him into this situation.
- **OTHER CHARACTERS' REACTIONS:** Clara makes it easy for us to figure out what's going on in the scene. She's terse, sharp, cold, accusatory—and clearly angry.
- **IMAGE CUES:** As soon as Clara confronts him, he's "out the window with the pigeons," a sign that he is mentally fleeing this awful moment. Then he compares her braids to "spinnakers on a tugboat"—an absurd image that conjures what might be called gallows laughter, or the sort of laughter that's a better alternative to crying.

These cues all add up to the surface feeling of regret. But subset feelings lurk beneath: dread, shame, and even a little indignation that he is the only one getting in trouble.

If you're bored with first person but you want to make your character as intimate as possible, or you want to speak to deeply human, universal truths, some variation of second person is probably for you!

NOW YOU

GET INTIMATE

Write a scene in which your protagonist is engaged in some sketchy behavior. But it can't be bad behavior for no reason; maybe she's just been jilted by a lover and is drinking her sorrows away, but has gotten too drunk for her own good and does something foolish, with ensuing consequences. Or perhaps your character lets anger get the best of him and calls someone out in a public setting, like his workplace or school, and that also results in consequences. In second-person intimate, describe the scene that unfolds.

Then rewrite the scene in either first person or third-person intimate. How does the scene feel different? Which version flows better? Which feels more true to character?

TELL A UNIVERSAL ASIDE

Write or revise a pivotal first person or third-person intimate scene, and drop into a universal aside in second person. Consider the theme of your story while doing this—these sorts of asides often lend themselves to thematic content. If your story is about recovering from trauma, pick a moment in the plot that is going to test and challenge your protagonist. A universal aside might be something like: "When you go out in public, you can't trust your surroundings to be free of loud noises and bright lights, the sort of thing that can trigger a panic attack."

GET OBSESSED

Write a scene in which your protagonist is obsessed with another character and following her without her notice. (Is it stalking or simply innocent adoration? It's your choice.) Have your narrator notice, observe, and comment, in second person and in his own mind, on everything the object of his obsession is doing, while talking himself into building up the nerve to approach the person. Add an element of danger, in which your narrator could get caught.

11

THE UNRELIABLE NARRATOR

The Perks and Perils of the Shifty Point of View

> *"Trust no friend without faults,*
> *and love a woman, but no angel."*

—DORIS LESSING

Well-written literature makes a tacit agreement between the author and readers that the characters in the book are trustworthy and will take them on a reliable journey. However, there exists a murky character known as "the unreliable narrator"—someone who tells the story but may obscure the whole truth, outright obfuscate, or purposely give only one side of the story to remain blameless. This type of narrator often reveals her unreliability up front, often in the form of contradictions, which forces readers to continue reading despite their initial misgivings. An unreliable narrator may also make grandiose claims, have psychic visions, hear voices, or display behavior that hints at mental instability.

Reliability is a matter of trust. Do readers trust the character, or don't they? And if they don't, are they willing to keep reading to find out more? It requires an interesting character or situation.

Not all fiction is about likable people going on a journey of redemption. Some novels exist to explore dark places in the human psyche, to understand what makes a murderer, to show what it's like to be caught in the grips of a mental illness. Often in those cases, the narrative needs an unreliable narrator to tell that story.

Unreliable narrators create tension on the page, and in the narrative itself, as readers wonder how this shifty character's story will play out. We all love a train wreck, and we get a vicarious thrill of being a fly on the wall of someone else's bad behavior—think of popular shows like *Breaking Bad* and *Californication*. But as with all well-constructed fiction, such a narrator must have a purpose and shouldn't exist just to amuse the writer. Furthermore, you must make clear to readers the motivation and history that at least partially justifies or explains the character's unreliability. Fiction breathes (though the reader doesn't) when tension is present—that indelible feeling, an urgency, even, that compels readers to keep reading because they must know more. Unreliable narrators are bastions of tension; they take readers captive, holding the keys to the car on a wild thrill ride that those readers won't abandon, even when they don't know where the hell they're going. When an unreliable narrator is rendered well, readers don't care that she can't be trusted, because they simply can't stop reading.

Let's look at how unreliable narrators work within the various points of view, and what cues allow readers to identify their reliability.

THE UNRELIABLE NARRATOR IN FIRST PERSON

First-person POV works particularly well with unreliable narrators, because a first-person story is filtered through only one character's point of view, biases, and beliefs, be they erroneous or wise. In other words, the reader has to take the first-person narrator's word for everything. A reader won't know that the narrator is untrustworthy if, or until, other characters shed the light of validity on the first-person narrator's story or discredit it outright.

In *The Virgins*, Pamela Erens employs a strategy I've seen only a few times in literature. Her first-person narrator, Bruce Bennett-Jones, narrates the stories of two other characters he meets at an elite boarding school, Aviva and Seung, with whom he becomes fixated, and whose stories intersect with his own in dramatic ways. But in sections where most authors would have chosen to break to a new scene and enter a new character's POV, Erens has Bruce imagine or re-create events that happened to Aviva or Seung. Bruce becomes the omniscient narrator, telling the reader information he doesn't likely know, which is perhaps the least reliable form of narration that exists. Let's take a look at our first introduction to Aviva, still in Bruce's first-person POV:

> She turns her ankle as she comes down the bus steps—just a little wobble—laughs, and rights herself again. Her sandals are tapered and high. Only a tiny heel connects with the rubber coated steps. She wears a silky purple dress, slit far up the side, and a white blazer. Her outfit is as strange in this place—this place of crewneck sweaters and Docksiders—as a clown's nose and paddle feet. Her eyes are heavily made up, blackened somehow, sleepy, deep …
>
> I jump up. Cort and Voss are still computing, trying to figure this girl out, but I don't intend to wait. Voss makes a popping sound with his lips, to mock me and to offer his respectful surprise. After all, I supposedly already have a girlfriend.
>
> "Do you need some help?" I ask her.
>
> She smiles slowly, theatrically. Her teeth are very straight, very white. Orthodontia or maybe fluoride in the water. I wonder where she's from. City, fancy suburb? I can see it in her dark eyes, the bump in her nose, her thick, dark kinky hair.

Bruce has already given us some cues of unreliability, subtle though they may be:

Writing the Intimate Character

- **INTERNAL MONOLOGUE CUES:** In his thoughts, he describes Aviva as strange—an outsider—and compares her to a clown. These are all negative assessments of her, yet he jumps up and offers to help her as though he is interested in her.
- **OTHER CHARACTERS' REACTIONS:** Voss raises an eyebrow because he knows that Bruce has a girlfriend and is suspicious of Bruce's actions in helping this girl. Though it may be harmless flirting, Bruce has spent quite a lot of time observing this girl's every physical detail and action, which suggests more than passing interest.

The passage continues:

> "I'm in Hiram," she says.
>
> Let me re-create her journey.
>
> She awakens in her big room at an hour when it is still dark, pushes open the curtains of her four-poster bed. Little princess. Across the hall, her brother is still sleeping. He's four years younger than she is: twelve.

It's at the line "Let me re-create her journey" where Bruce's reliability comes intently into question. Telling Aviva's story as though it is his own plants further doubt about his character. How can we trust that the story he tells is really Aviva's? We can't, but through the magic of fiction we stop asking that question long enough to let the story unfold. Later in the book he also narrates: "I'm inventing Seung, too, of course. It's the least I can do for him." In much the same way that the unreliable narrator Humbert Humbert, in Nabokov's *Lolita*, tells his version of the story about his inappropriate relationship with his stepdaughter in order to make himself seem like an innocent victim, Bruce takes ownership of Aviva's and Seung's stories and spins them for the reader as though to suggest that he was, perhaps, a victim of circumstances rather than responsible for his own behavior. While it's an unorthodox way of playing with POV, it matches Bruce's character. As the novel unfolds we learn more and more how selfish he is, how diabolical, how obsessed in his attention.

In fact, obsession is a common theme in stories with unreliable narrators. The novel *Perfume* by Patrick Süskind is narrated by a serial killer, a perfumer in the eighteenth century who is trying to preserve and re-create the scent of his victims as a perfume. He is the ultimate antihero, unreliable because he is a murderer. Yet by inviting readers to see the world through his eyes, we can put aside our misgivings to attempt to understand him. The unreliable narrator can be used to guide readers into the darkest parts of human nature so that they may investigate them.

THE UNRELIABLE NARRATOR IN SECOND PERSON

Since it's the rare novel that is written entirely in the second-person POV, there isn't a huge body of work from which to draw. You may find yourself flying blind if you do write in this POV. However, one unforgettable and chilling contemporary example is Caroline Kepnes's thriller, *You*, which I introduced in chapter ten. The book's protagonist, Joe, is a classic antihero, a character who commits despicable, criminal acts and has no chance for redemption. And yet he does not see himself this way at all. He's so unreliable that not only does he lie to other characters as well as to readers, he frequently lies to himself. He has all the hallmarks of a sociopath: He sees people as objects, lacks emotional depth, and goes to whatever lengths he must to get what he wants and thinks he deserves.

From the very first page, when Joe spots Beck, a young, attractive girl who walks in to shop at the bookstore where he works, Joe reveals himself as unreliable:

> You walk into the bookstore and you keep your hand on the door to make sure it doesn't slam. You smile, embarrassed to be a nice girl, and your nails are bare and your V-neck sweater is beige and it's impossible to know if you're wearing a bra but I don't think that you are. …
>
> You are classic and compact, my own little Natalie Portman circa the end of the movie *Closer*, when she's fresh-faced and done

with the bad British guys and going home to America. You've come home to me, delivered at last on a Tuesday, 10:06 A.M. Every day I commute to this shop on the Lower East Side from my place in Bed-Stuy. Every day I close up without finding anyone like you. Look at you, born into my world today. I'm shaking and I'd pop an Ativan but they're downstairs and I don't want to pop an Ativan. I don't want to come down. I want to be here, fully, watching you bite your unpainted nails and turn your head to the left. ...

Let's look at the internal monologue cues that show the narrator's unreliability. From the moment Beck walks through the door, Joe makes internal observations about her that he can't possibly know. He assumes she keeps her hand on the door so it doesn't slam. He assumes her smile is one of embarrassment. These do not show him to be a reliable judge of character, though we don't yet assume anything more. But then, some of his thoughts sound quite narcissistic, if not alarming. He claims her as "my own little Natalie Portman" and, most alarming, he thinks, "You've come home to me" and "born into my world today." These suggest someone who is unstable and inappropriately possessive, but the reader holds onto the benefit of the doubt; he could just be melodramatic.

Through a series of well-orchestrated manipulations and maneuvers, Joe gets to know Beck, and they begin casually dating, though Beck is still hung up on an ex-boyfriend and never wants to fully commit to Joe.

In order to preserve his sense of self, when things don't go as he wants Joe simply revises or rewrites the story. It's fascinating to witness these revisions unfold. In the following scene, Beck has been avoiding Joe after a date that went somewhat badly. But when she asks him to go with her to IKEA to buy a new bed and help her assemble it, he quickly spins the request as renewed faith in her "love" for him:

Upon learning that assemblymen do not double as slaves, you reached out to me:

Do you like Ikea? Hint hint.

It goes without saying that I don't like IKEA. But of course I wrote back:

Love it actually. Go there every day. Why?

It's not romantic and it's a daylight date but I understand that your attraction to me is so intense that you need to keep a safe distance. That's why you wrote back:

Want to get on the boat with me? There will be meatballs.

Meatballs is a sexless word and the boat is actually a ferry that goes to IKEA. Furniture shopping is a thankless task but you murmured I like you about a thousand times in the cab after Peach's party and those murmurings trump whatever bullshit you spew to your friends on Twitter.

No meatballs required, but I'll get on a boat with you.

Notice the way he spins rejection into attraction with the line "but I understand that your attraction to me is so intense that you need to keep a safe distance." Throughout the book Joe warps reality for the version he prefers in his head. The more Joe convinces himself that Beck's lackluster displays of interest in him actually reflect love and intensity, the more he can justify his bad behavior to come. In fact, this process is so organic to Joe's personality that we get the feeling he isn't justifying his behavior at all—he never actually sees reality for what it is. Thus, as the story unfolds, we understand that he is not someone to be trusted. Certainly readers are likely to begin reading with curiosity about this overly confident fellow and keep reading to see how this train wreck resolves. The contrast between Joe's version of reality and Beck's creates a taut and unending tension as he continually manufactures ways to possess Beck and spin the world toward his own agenda.

THE UNRELIABLE NARRATOR IN OMNISCIENT

It is quite hard to pull off an unreliable narrator in the omniscient POV because the nature of this viewpoint is authoritative and all-knowing. This narrator is not bound by the personal hang-ups and baggage of an individual; she can move beyond the boundaries of human space and time, as well as with much less emotion, and is likely to feel impersonal. Though you can zoom from the external omniscient POV to the internal third-person intimate (at which point you could certainly have a limited, unreliable narrator), unreliable omniscience poses greater storytelling challenges.

THE UNRELIABLE NARRATOR IN THIRD-PERSON INTIMATE

Third-person intimate is as effective for an unreliable narrator as first person, because once again you can take only the viewpoint character's words or thoughts as evidence. One of my favorite unreliable third-person narrators is Miriam Black, the smack-talking, nomadic female protagonist of Chuck Wendig's titular series. We meet Miriam in the first book, *Blackbirds*, in a seedy hotel room with a man named Del Amico. All we know about Del is that he is a truck driver and has picked up Miriam from a truck stop. Del believes that Miriam is a prostitute, though she quickly tells him she is not. Whenever a character says she is not who she appears to be, it points to unreliability. The scene does not unfold as Del—or readers, for that matter—anticipate. We are left to wonder who Miriam is and why she's in the hotel with him. Her unreliability becomes evident when she begins to taunt him, suggesting that he is about to meet the end of his life:

> "Since we're waiting, I should *probably* also tell you that I've been following you for a couple weeks now." His gaze narrows again, and he's looking at her like maybe he recognizes her, or is trying to. She keeps talking. "I know you like hookers. Pros and hos. All kinds, too! You're the kind of fellow who'll eat every candy out of the chocolate box. Variety is the spice of life, good for you. I *also* happen to know that, outside of some relatively boring sexual proclivities, you like to hit women. Four prostitutes. Two with black eyes, one with a cut chin, the fourth with a busted lower lip. …"
>
> Del moves fast.

Bam. A tight coiled fist hits her right in the eye and knocks her back on the bed. Capillaries burst. Fireworks on a black background. Gasping, she scrambles backward, thinking he's going to advance and try to beat her or choke her, but by the time she's in a crouch and ready to kick, bite, or collapse his throat with a forearm, she sees he hasn't moved one inch.

He's just standing there. Shaking. Angry, sad, confused; she can't tell. She waits it out. He doesn't move toward her. He isn't even looking at her now—Del's staring off at a nowhere point a thousand miles from here.

Gingerly, Miriam reaches over to the nightstand and turns the alarm clock so she can read it. It's an old-ass clock, the kind with the numbers that turn like Vanna White's flipping them. Each with a *click*.

"It's 12.40," she says. "That means you have three minutes."

"Three minutes?" He narrows his gaze, trying to suss out her game.

"That's right, Del, three minutes. Now's the time to ask yourself: Any thoughts you want to share? Grandma's cornbread recipe? Location of a buried pirate treasure? Any poetic last words? You know, *either the wallpaper goes, or I do*?" She waves him off. "I know, an Oscar Wilde reference. I reached too far for that one. My bad."

He doesn't move, but he tightens up. Every muscle pulled taut to bone.

"You think you're going to kill me?" he asks. "*That* what you think?"

She clucks her tongue. "No, sir, I do not think that. I'm not the killer type. I'm more *passive* aggressive than aggressive. I'm a *wait and see* kind of girl. More vulture than falcon."

They stare at each other. She feels scared and sick and a little excited.

Click.

The 0 flips to 1.

"You want to hit me again," she says.

"I just might."

I'll save the rest of this scene for you to read yourself, but notice the tension created by the many contradictions in what Miriam says and thinks. There are multiple ways to create that kind of tension, but in Miriam Black's case, unreliability is a big part of her character and thus a useful tension-generating tool. Her backstory is revealed over the course of the series, showing us how she can neither trust nor be trusted, but she makes for a fun and punchy narrator in a series of compelling stories.

Let's look at some of the unreliability cues in this scene:

- **INTERNAL MONOLOGUE CUES:** In the narrative voice of Miriam's thoughts, we learn that she has been following Del Amico for a couple of weeks. Why would a reliable person do that unless she's some kind of private investigator? (As far as we know, she's not.) At the beginning of the scene, we don't know her true intentions, but her unreliability is not a deal breaker—she redeems this bad behavior by having a certain bent toward justice, or at least against guys who beat women. This makes her likable, even though she's not yet trustworthy.
- **DIALOGUE CUES:** Miriam's sarcastic dialogue belies the seriousness of the situation. She's cornered a strange man in a hotel room after rolling out a list of his crimes, but even after he punches her, she doesn't seem afraid. Instead she calls his attention to the clock by moving it toward him and pointing at the time (a small physical-action cue). Later in the excerpt, another dialogue cue contradicts what seems likely: She's just told Del Amico he's going to die, but she also tells him she won't kill him: "I'm not the killer type. I'm more *passive* aggressive than aggressive. I'm a *wait and see* kind of girl. More vulture than falcon." It's hard to trust what she's saying, but we can't look away either.

Another way to make an unreliable narrator compelling is to place him in a sticky situation or make him take actions that can't be undone. Fiction thrives on conflict, and the characters most likely to get into trouble are often the most unreliable. Donald Maass, literary agent and author of several great writing guides, writes the following in a blog post for the website Writer Unboxed:

> Human beings can be broken into two broad psychological categories: those who store tension and those who store energy. Those things may sound the same but they're not. People who store tension turn inward. Those who store energy turn outward. The first group ponders, reflects, thinks, and feels. The latter group acts. One set of people likes to deal with life over a cup of tea with a splash of conversation. The other set prefers to go for a run or smack a ball with a stick.

Miriam Black is a great example of a character who turns outward and acts. The more you can have a character act without explaining, thinking, or hesitating, the more likely the reader is to come along for the ride. With an unreliable narrator, you should keep a reader hooked even more than with other kinds of characters.

BECOMING RELIABLE

Depending on your character's story arc, your unreliable narrator may *become* reliable by the end of your tale, particularly if yours is a redemption story or if your character's plot involves a significant emotional transformation. Although, consider this side note: In series fiction, characters often transform far less dramatically from book to book, because the point of a series is familiarity with a character. Keep in mind that unreliable narrators who commit terrible crimes like murder or rape will be harder to redeem. Joe, the protagonist of *You*, would need prison, church, therapy, and probably a lifetime of community service to come back from his darkness. He remains unreliable to the end. Miriam Black, on the other hand, has room to grow—she's the type of person whose unreliability may stem from wounds that can heal, and, with time, she can learn to trust and become trustworthy. You should, of course, consider these details in the plot-planning stage of your novel, which we will discuss further in chapter twelve.

CONSIDERATIONS FOR CREATING AN UNRELIABLE NARRATOR

Throughout this chapter we've looked at several hallmarks of the unreliable narrator. When crafting your own, consider giving her the following:

- **CONTRADICTIONS**: Unreliable narrators are full of contradictions. They say one thing but think another; they reveal partial information or refuse to reveal something outright. The more contradictions you create, the less reliable your narrator will seem.
- **A TROUBLED PAST**: Some unreliable narrators are inherently good characters who have learned untrustworthy behavior as a matter of self-defense or self-preservation. This might be a kid who grew up in foster care, a former concubine, an orphan in a foreign land, or any number of abuse victims. These unreliable narrators can often be redeemed by overcoming their past, healing, meeting people who recognize the good in them, or acting on behalf of others.
- **OBSESSION**: Many stories deal with obsession in one form or another. You could argue that *Romeo and Juliet* is a tale of obsessive young love. Not all obsession must become dark and deadly, but oftentimes it skews a person's thinking or beliefs. If your protagonist is in the grip of obsession, be aware that she may come off as unreliable, whether or not you intend this.

Writing unreliable narrators can be a lot of fun. Not all fiction has to be about honest, wholesome, easy-to-understand people. There's no harm in exploring the complexities of the human psyche on the page.

NOW YOU

DO AS I SAY, NOT AS I DO

In first person, create an unreliable character who is inherently good but comes across as unreliable because of his contradictory behavior (which could be a result of fear or doubt). Write a scene in which your character says one thing but does another. Using the reactions of other characters, show that this makes your character seem unreliable.

REINTERPRETATION

Using third-person intimate, put your character in a situation where she faces rejection. Rather than allow her to feel rejected, have your character rewrite the story in her own mind to reflect an inaccurate reading of the situation that makes her believe she has not been rejected.

Writing the Intimate Character

PART THREE
Stretch Your Skills

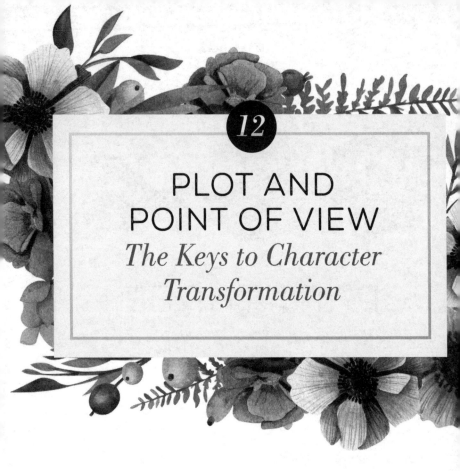

12

PLOT AND POINT OF VIEW
The Keys to Character Transformation

> *"Get your character in trouble in the first sentence and out of trouble in the last sentence."*
>
> **—BARTHE DECLEMENTS**

So far in this book we've looked at point of view as the camera or lens for the story you're telling and the proximity by which readers connect with your characters. POV is also important to character development because it allows you to experience unique internal landscapes and explore people who are not you—which can help you create good art and good entertainment. Now we'll look at what makes characters compelling and stories revelatory: character transformation. This is the way you show how the events of your plot affect your character, and vice versa, as your character's emotional and mental states also create consequences that lead to future plot events.

In our book *Writing Deep Scenes*, my co-author Martha Alderson writes the following:

> In all stories, to one degree or another, plot is how the dramatic events (action) in a story change and/or transform the main character (emotion) over time in a meaningful way (theme). The degree of character change or transformation can vary dramatically depending on the genre.

As a result of events and their consequences, your character should be forced to change, either emotionally or spiritually, as is often found in literary fiction, or with a smaller, simpler epiphany, understanding, or conclusion of a mystery or question, as in genre fiction.

But why is transformation so important? Why does it matter? You might be thinking, *I've read plenty of good books where nobody changes.* To this I'll say: What do you remember about those books, if anything? We enjoy good stories that don't have any character change, but we *remember* books with powerful transformations.

Stories reflect, edify, and illuminate the life lessons we are taught in our own lives: forgiveness, redemption, great love, and so on. Plots, however, are a sweetened, condensed version of life: They are a life lesson or a major change compressed into a few hundred pages, giving readers relatively quick lessons compared to the lessons learned in real life.

The vehicle for both dramatic events and character change is the *scene*—in which you use more real-time action and sensory imagery than summary or thoughts to show events and the character's reactions to them.

WHAT IS A SCENE?

At its most essential, a scene is a simulation of real moments that expand a story from one dimension into three in the minds of your readers. Every scene needs the following:

- physical action to mimic time passing and show characters demonstrating behavior
- sensory imagery to fully flesh out the scene and incorporate readers' senses
- setting details to plant readers (and the character) in physical space
- dialogue, when appropriate to the plot, to let characters reveal themselves and their intentions
- plot information—a consequence or revelation from a prior scene that pushes the story forward

Without action, there's no scene. And there are some other considerations about scenes you should be aware of. If you switch from one POV character to another while using any of the intimate POVs (first person, second person, or third-person intimate, as discussed in Part Two), you *must* change scenes. That means you will need to end the scene in Character A's POV and start a new one in Character B's, thus dropping into a new character's mind. (This is only when you have multiple protagonists.) If you are using omniscient POV, you have the freedom to move between characters' minds in the same scene, and they need not all be major characters.

Ultimately, the recipe for strong, well-rounded, believable characters is a combination of practice and time. You might get a few elements right in the first draft but need to attend to others in later drafts based on beta-reader feedback. As long as you are open to going deeper and exploring the nuances of viewpoint and character development, you'll be well on your way.

Good plots exist upon a framework of tension, in which the fate of a character is often up in the air, uncertain, and unfolding throughout the course of the book. Readers continue to read because they have to know what happens next. You can keep that tension alive by not giving away all the plot elements up front, and by doling them out in bits instead.

HOW POV AFFECTS YOUR PLOT

So how does the POV you choose influence the plot and your character's transformation? To understand this we must hark back to our discussion of intimacy. How close do you want to let readers get to your character's experience? Are they watching from an omniscient distance or from a deeply intimate first-person viewpoint?

Epic plots that span wide swaths of time often benefit from the omniscient POV, which can fill in bits of history and information that the characters themselves may not know, while also offering context to the reader. However, personal stories of loss and love are often more evocative in the intimate, internal POVs because they allow readers to merge with the character. Stories of great pain and suffering may be better executed in the third-person intimate, which offers some distance to help readers assimilate what they're reading.

Let's briefly revisit the main ways to demonstrate character emotion (and thus change) in the context of plot:

- **ACTION CUES:** Action cues are the universal language of all POVs and a necessary ingredient for any plot. Plot events unfold as characters act, engage, and move through space and time. Readers can "see" someone thrusting open a door, kicking an attacker, digging the treasure out of the ground, or pulling a lover close for a kiss. Regardless of how intimate your POV, these cues require no translation; they are simple and universal. They are also the quickest way to create the sensation of real time passing. The kinds of action you write also reflect the internal landscape of your characters. The manner in which a character acts can speak volumes about how he feels.

- **DIALOGUE CUES:** As with action cues, you can use spoken words to reveal crucial plot information to readers. It's vastly more effective to have a character show emotion or unveil a plot discovery through speech than to keep that same feeling or revelation solely in the realm of internal monologue.

- **SENSORY IMAGERY CUES:** Sometimes words and actions fail or can't be used to convey a character's reaction to what is happening around her. What's more, readers want to know what your characters are feeling in reaction to the plot events. When your protagonist is kidnapped, is she scared or angry? When she loses or gains something, what emotions arise inside her? Sensory imagery—that which is felt in the body as a manifestation of feelings—offers vital information about the character's internal landscape and informs the actions she will take next.

- **INTERNAL MONOLOGUE CUES:** Though you always want to limit your use of thoughts because they slow down the forward movement of the plot, thoughts do reflect a character's state of mind. To flatly summarize a character's feelings, save thoughts for times when characters might not otherwise be able to verbalize, or for memories of past plot events that lead to epiphanies as the character pieces together vital information.

- **OTHER CHARACTERS' REACTIONS:** Finally, remember that your protagonist will rarely change or achieve a goal alone—other characters will almost always support and oppose your protagonist. These people also provide foils against which your protagonist's flaws are tested and his strengths are realized. Caring about other characters, working on behalf of them, and fighting for and against them shows readers what your protagonist is made of. And in so doing, the reactions of those other characters reveal as much about how your character is changing as does his own behavior.

Stories Are Driven by the Unknown

In chapter five we talked about the limits of character self-awareness. At the beginning, your character shouldn't be so self-aware that he has little to no room for growth. The same goes for the events of the plot—don't give away too much too soon. Once you learn to work with plot design or structure, however, you'll quickly understand that events in a character's life must unfold in a certain order. This order is driven by two factors:

1. what your character needs in order to move to the next emotional stage, which determines the plot event you'll work with next
2. the pressures the antagonists pose upon the protagonist

Looking Forward or Looking Back

Some stories are told retrospectively; that is, the character has already lived through an experience and is recounting it to another character (and thus to readers). In this case, be careful not to reveal too much of the story too soon, since the narrator already knows everything that happened.

More often, readers are along for the ride, moment by moment, with a character who is looking ahead to an unresolved future. This makes for a more compelling tale, because neither character nor reader knows what will happen next, creating necessary page-turning tension.

Often in the looking-forward style of storytelling, you will jump briefly back in time with flashbacks to allow readers to understand a scene from the past. In the looking-back format, make sure to serve this information cautiously so that the whole story doesn't unspool too soon, like a sweater thread caught on a nail.

CHARACTER TRANSFORMATION AND THE ENERGETIC MARKERS

Martha Alderson coined the term *energetic markers* to describe the essential components of plot design. These markers are pivot points at which external events (action) create internal reactions (emotion) inside the character and force change.

The four energetic markers are as follows:

1. **POINT OF NO RETURN:** At the first quarter mark of your plot, this is where your character is called to adventure or change. Once this happens, they can't easily return to their old life or reality.
2. **REDEDICATION:** This marker occurs at the midpoint of the book, where your protagonist must look past fears and push forward to move on with the plot.
3. **DARK NIGHT:** At the three-quarter mark of your plot, your character undergoes devastating dramatic action that leads to crisis, death, or loss.
4. **TRIUMPH:** Just near the end of your book is the most intense scene of the story, both emotionally and in terms of dramatic action. Protagonist and antagonist are at equal power, but the protagonist achieves a hard-won victory because of the confidence and maturity she has earned during the story.

As we go through this section, keep in mind how differently these energetic markers might look depending on the POV and intimacy of the character.

The Beginning: Setting the Stage for Character Change

A story should begin with your character in the "shadows." In this state of uncertainty, your character knows little about the world, the story, and herself, including her own inner strengths and flaws. This lack of knowledge is important to the plot because it drives both character and reader curiosity. The beginning is a time of introductions, and you must be careful in how you write it. Readers need enough detail to be hooked by the story and the character, but not so much backstory or so many plot points that they become overwhelmed or bored.

Let's look at the beginning of Elizabeth Little's novel *Dear Daughter*, whose opening lines introduce us to the first-person POV of Jane Jenkins. Jane has just been released after only ten years into a life sentence in prison for murdering her famous mother. New evidence has come to light that her case was mishandled, causing the judge to overturn her conviction. Jane believes she is innocent, or at least she has no memory of murdering her mother. As the story unfolds, we learn Jane's case was high profile and that it still receives a great deal of media attention since the public is "overwhelmingly convinced of Jenkins's guilt."

> But I never meant for it to come to this. There's attention and then there's *attention*, and sure, the latter gets you fame and money and free designer shoes, but I'm not Lindsay Lohan. I understand the concept of declining marginal returns. It was the not knowing—that's what I couldn't stand. That's why I'm here …

The Emotional Set-Point: Setting the Trajectory for Character Change

At the beginning, the author provides a snapshot of Jane's state of mind. Think of this as the character's "set-point"—the starting gate for her emotional arc. This set-point will change by story's end and will also serve to launch the engine for the plot.

Once she gets out of prison, Jane feels it is foolish to stick around the city of her release, considering that people wish her dead. And yet, like the reader, she can't stand not knowing what happened:

> Imagine how it would feel if, out of the blue, someone were to hand you a gold medal and tell you it was yours. *Oh my god*, you'd think. *I am so super awesome! I won the Olympics. But, wait—what did I win? When did I win it? When did I train?*
>
> Now imagine that instead of a gold medal you were given a murder conviction, and you'll have some sense of how it is for me.
>
> When I think back on the night my mother died, it's like trying to adjust a pair of rabbit ears to pick up a distant broadcast signal. Every so often something comes into focus, but mostly I just get the scrape-sound of static, an impenetrable wall of snow …
>
> It's hard enough to maintain your innocence when so many people are so sure you're not. It's impossible when you're not sure of anything at all—other than the awful, inescapable fact that you hadn't particularly liked your own mother …

Of all the challenges of incarceration, this was perhaps the worst: I was fundamentally a rational creature reduced to rudimentary divination. I promised myself that if I ever got out I'd try to find out what really happened, to find out what I really was.

Since the vast majority of this information is delivered in narrative summary, without dialogue or action, we have to parse through what she's telling us to find the imagistic cues in this scene. The Olympics analogy is an image that conveys a feeling, in this case shock, befuddlement, and confusion. Then we get more—"like trying to adjust a pair of rabbit ears" and "the scrape-sound of static"—which demonstrate that her memories are unclear. She doesn't know what happened to her mother.

We learn other information at the beginning of the novel in literal facts reported to us directly:

- She has just been released from prison, where she served ten years of her original life sentence for her mother's murder.
- She does not remember committing that murder and doubts that it was her, but DNA evidence found on the scene suggested otherwise.
- She didn't like her mother, which is a potential motive for the crime.
- She doesn't want the media attention she will surely receive if she sticks around.
- She *must* stick around and find out who killed her mother, because she can't live her life without knowing the truth—even if it turns out to be a dark truth about herself.

All of this information (delivered in about three pages) provides an emotional set-point we might call "confused but determined," or "uncertain but motivated." This set-point offers a trajectory for Jane's character to transform through the energetic markers of the plot. By the end of the novel Jane should no longer be confused because she'll be informed. She won't need to be determined anymore, either, because she'll have answers about the identity of her mother's killer. The emotional set-point also provides the catalyst for the plot. Jane now has a directive, a goal: to find out who killed her mother. To find out why. In this process she might also come to terms with the mother she didn't like very much, and learn more about why she felt this way.

When creating the emotional set-point for your character, consider the following:

- What event haunts your character? (This could be a trauma, a secret, a loss, or a failure). What cues can you use to convey this without narrative summary?
- What is your character's emotional landscape (i.e., guilty, sad, lonely, angry)? What cues best demonstrate this?
- What action(s) will your character take, based on the above two factors, to set this story in motion? It should have sufficient emotional intensity and stakes to act as a Point of No Return.
- What is the trajectory of change for your character? How must he become different by the end of the story to reflect his growth? What are the cues that will demonstrate this growth?

At each energetic marker, your character must demonstrate growth through her actions and words, and even her thoughts. Between each marker, remember that characters should be continually tested and pushed. While she may gain small rewards, don't let her coast along and get comfy. Compress the carbon of your characters into diamonds by putting them through extreme stress and conflict.

Point of No Return: Activating Character Change

The story really begins when your character takes an action or makes a decision that can't easily be undone. This moment should not be subtle and is most effective when fraught with complex emotions. Some writers refer to this marker as the "Call to Adventure," but it can just as easily be called the "Pressure to Change." It's the first, most important plot point in your story, and it marks the last moment at which your character remains who he was at the beginning. Change is now imminent.

In *Dear Daughter*, Jane appealed to a lawyer named Noah while she was in prison, and Noah developed an unhealthy affection for her that works in her favor. At the beginning of the book, he is the only person to whom Jane reveals her post-release whereabouts, as the media is already slavering to get wind of her, and people who believe she is guilty are making death threats over the Internet. Noah gets her a fake ID with a new name—Rebecca Parker—and brings her hair dye and scissors to change her appearance. He doesn't like her plan to disappear—he thinks doing so would make her look guilty, and he has always believed in her innocence—but he doesn't know that she plans to try and solve the case. Changing her identity and then leaving town is Jane's Point of No Return, the first major energetic shift in the story, where she takes action that will set all the remaining plot events, and thus her own transformation, in motion.

Since first person is an intimate, internal POV, we must look for signs of her character transformation mostly through her spoken words and physical actions, and through the reactions of other characters to her. If this were written in an omniscient POV, character transformation would have to be revealed through external narrative asides and philosophical musings as well as through the observations of other characters.

Rededication: Deepening Character Commitment

Once a character launches into his journey, things will become more complicated, and eventually complications, often at the hands of the antagonist(s), will lead to an understandable resistance in his will to move forward. This resistance may take the form of fear, fatigue, doubt, insecurity, and many other emotions. But to complete a plot journey, your character *has* to move forward. Overcoming this resistance at this juncture brings us to the second energetic marker,

Rededication. This important pivot point is where your character rallies some inner strength, the support of an ally, or pure willpower to push on.

In *Dear Daughter*, this moment is Jane's arrival at the small town of Ardelle, South Dakota—the only link she has to her mother's cryptic past. The state of the town so clashes with Jane's perception of her wealthy, elegant mother that she nearly gives up on the search and turns back.

> Something was wilting in the vicinity of my chest. I mean, seriously? *This* place? What connection could my mother possibly have to a town like this? She was as fastidious with her surroundings as she was with her attire, because she knew that even a D-flawless diamond looks like crap in a 10K setting. She had even considered *Beverly Hills* to be beneath her.

But Jane has nowhere else to go. She presses ahead, despite her doubts. It marks the beginning of Jane's emotional change, as she is now forced to consider that there was more to her mother than she realized:

> I turned and headed toward the inn. One thing made sense, at least: if my mother had known someone who lived here, no way would she have ever admitted it.

Rededication in first person and the other intimate viewpoints is likely to come in two main forms: (1) The protagonist makes a declaration aloud to someone else that she is going forward with a plan or getting back on the path, or (2) the protagonist makes a decision in the form of internal monologue along the lines of Jane's choice above.

In omniscient, Rededication may be narrated to the reader: "And so Jane pressed ahead into the dark night, determined to show how brave she was."

Dark Night: Stripping Away the False

The Dark Night, the third energetic marker, is the low point of your protagonist's journey, the place of seeming failure, where the antagonists appear to reign supreme and your protagonist is at her most defeated. This is often a place of literal death, the betrayal of an ally, or the death of a belief or hope that your character held until this point. Although this marker brings a loss of some kind, it also marks the beginning of great maturity and emotional change for your protagonist. Once all has been lost, your character gains crystal clarity and truth, and usually some form of determination.

For Jane, this comes in two parts: (1) the online gossip blogger Trace Kessler, who has been tracking down clues of her whereabouts since her release from prison, figures out where she is, and (2) Jane learns that her mother, known as Marion Elsinger but actually born as Tessa Kanty, was not who she purported to be. Jane learns that her own existence may have been the result of a crime of passion in which Tessa committed murder.

Though this information is unpleasant, even devastating, it's the truth, and it helps Jane relate to her mother in an entirely new way.

Dark Nights revealed in first person can feel even more devastating or harsh because readers are right inside the character. This is important to consider in stories that deal with painful, intense subjects and radical character transformation; the more intimate the POV, the greater the emotional impact on your reader. Not every story needs to be that close to the character's internal experience.

Triumph: Change Is Achieved

By the Triumph (sometimes known as the climax of the novel), your character's emotional shift or epiphany must be clear to the reader. You can make this change evident through actions your character takes that he couldn't before; through the confidence in or use of skills he didn't know he had; and through positive dialogue that expresses conviction, faith, or purpose. There's no longer a question of *how* your character will change, because that change is clearly in motion, and it helps him achieve his goal, vanquish the antagonist, and emerge triumphant.

Every Triumph will be different. Here, the protagonist achieves his goals, reveals the antagonists as cowards and defeats them, and comes into his full power or awareness. In *Dear Daughter*, Jane learns the identity of her biological father and the truth of the murder that sent her mother fleeing, as well as the truth she needs to exonerate herself for her own mother's murder. She no longer has to live a lie, hide from the public eye, or define herself by her mother's secrets. The future is a blank slate of possibility.

At the Triumph, first person and other intimate POVs can heighten the feeling of victory and allow the reader to feel the vicarious joy and relief the protagonist feels at this high point of the story.

However, it's important to note that no matter what POV you use, from the most external and omniscient to the most tightly intimate, most characters must still undergo this four-part journey through the energetic markers to come across as believably transformed. Your work is to determine just how close you want the reader to be to that process through the POV you choose.

DEFINING THE SCOPE OF CHARACTER CHANGE

Character change takes place across a vast continuum of human experience. Some characters undergo a softer, quieter kind of transformation. The characters in series novels often see less character change per individual book, but over the course of the series they draw a definite, noticeable arc.

In genres like mysteries and thrillers, your character's transformation may simply be an understanding that allows her to figure out whodunit and why—most great mysteries find a way to connect the protagonist intimately with the case so that solving it comes with personal implications. In romance novels, the two lovers must usually overcome some personal obstacle or transform in some way so they can be together. Fantasy and science fiction novels, on the other hand, often show a meek, humble, or downtrodden character pressed to rise to heroic heights to save a people, a planet, a kingdom, or a crucial piece of technology. Transformation can be as simple as a person leaving an abusive marriage or as dramatic as a character discovering heroic qualities within.

While many perfectly good stories thrive without dramatic character change, it is a satisfying element that leaves readers feeling profoundly moved. On some level we all want to believe we have a chance at becoming the best version of ourselves, and fiction offers that possibility in the characters with whom we connect.

And, of course, the camera you choose for your POV will either drop readers right inside the avatar of your character or offer them a balcony seat at a distance, both of which have their advantages.

NOW YOU

SHAPE THE ARC

Answer the following questions about your character:

- What is your character haunted by as your story opens? It may be something deeply suppressed in her subconscious or a more overt wound that she can't get past.
- What is your character's emotional set-point at the beginning?
- How must your character change by the Triumph to reflect transformation?
- What happens to your character at the four energetic markers of your plot? Include both the plot event and the emotional change that happens inside your character.

THE ROOT OF CHANGE

Sum up your character's transformation in a couple of sentences that speak to the plot events. Here's an example from *Dear Daughter*:

> Spoiled former socialite is sent to prison for murdering her mother. Her journey to exonerate herself brings her to the small-town family she never knew, and to a greater understanding of her humble roots and her mother's love.

       Writing the Intimate Character

Then sum up your character's emotional change. Again, here's an example:

Learning the truth about her mother's past frees Jane from hate.

Remember, too, that you demonstrate your character's emotional state with every word he speaks or thinks, and with every action he takes. So when in doubt about how to take a snapshot of your character's emotional state, return to the character cues introduced in chapter four.

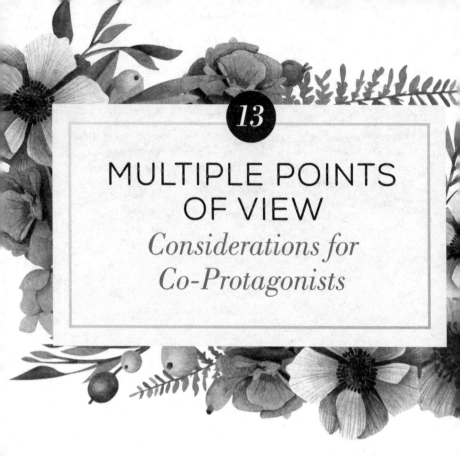

MULTIPLE POINTS OF VIEW
Considerations for Co-Protagonists

"It is a narrow mind which cannot look at a subject from various points of view."

—GEORGE ELIOT, *MIDDLEMARCH*

Some stories require greater scope, more voices, or a different context than can be delivered through the eyes of one protagonist. When you find this to be the case, consider using multiple viewpoints. However, you must think about several factors before launching into this greater undertaking. This chapter will walk you through the fine points of multiple POVs.

THE HALLMARKS OF MULTIPLE VIEWPOINTS

In a book with co-protagonists, each character should get approximately equal story weight. In other words, no one character is more important than the other, though one character's story may seem to drive the action more than the others. Usually these multiples are written in an intimate POV, and each co-protagonist gets his or her own POV chapter or scene, in which we are privy only to that character's thoughts and feelings. When your co-protagonists appear in a scene together, you still must choose which character's POV to show it from. This has the potential to get confusing, so remember to imagine that each character possesses a movie camera. The POV comes from the person whose camera (mind) we're looking through.

Using co-protagonists is different from omniscience, in which the POV can move between the heads of multiple characters in the same scene. Often in omniscient, the story has one protagonist, but the narrator still dips in and out of other characters' thoughts, adding flavor, clues, and color. But ultimately we are still following only the transformational arc of one character.

CONSIDERATIONS FOR CHOOSING MULTIPLE VIEWPOINTS

Using multiple viewpoints can benefit your story in several ways. Keep in mind that when showing the vantage points of co-protagonists in one of the intimate POVs, you must start a new scene or chapter each time you switch.

Here are some reasons to use multiple viewpoints in your novel:

- **YOURS IS A STORY THAT MUST BE TOLD FROM MANY PERSPEC-TIVES.** No matter how compelling one person's journey, some stories are more deeply realized when several people tell the same story, adding different facets to the larger picture. Novels that have done this include *All the Light We Cannot See* by Anthony Doerr, *The Girl on the Train* by Paula Hawkins, *The Help* by Kathryn Stockett, and *The Hours* by Michael Cunningham. This is especially true when each member in your cast of characters provides a unique piece to a larger puzzle: They might not understand each other's lives, or they might clash against one another as a result of plot events.

- **EACH CHARACTER OFFERS A UNIQUE PLOT THREAD OR STRAND TO THE STORY.** Multiple POVs only work when each POV character has a truly different story element to offer. They contribute new information, opinions, history, and clues that walk us deeper into the story's heart.

- **EACH CHARACTER IS COMPELLING AND HAS HIS OWN NARRATIVE ARC.** Sometimes writers confuse secondary or supporting characters for co-protagonists. A true co-protagonist must have his own narrative arc. He must be driven by his own unique goals and undergo a journey of transformation related to the larger plot. That's a lot harder to do than just maintaining one character's arc.

- **YOUR STORY SPANS A WIDE SWATH OF TIME AND HISTORY.** Historical novels or stories that cover large time periods often feel limited when told in only one character's POV. Since one character may also possess only a portion of the knowledge you need to convey, multiple characters can offer a feeling of depth and richness. But again, don't bring in a new co-protagonist unless you are sure she is integral to the plot and carries her own arc.

- **YOUR BOOK REQUIRES A QUICK AND COMPELLING PLOT PACE.** Multiple-character POVs have the power to make readers turn pages at a fast clip. As you end one character's compelling scene at an unresolved point, you also create a yearning in readers to know what happens next. Repeat this technique with two or three characters and you create positive page-turning tension.

MISTAKES WITH MULTIPLE VIEWPOINTS

Before you get too excited about creating a cast of co-characters, it's wise to consider some of the potential pitfalls inherent to multiple POVs:

- **READERS DON'T NEED THE POV OF THE ANTAGONIST UNLESS YOU'RE REDEEMING THAT ANTAGONIST VIA HIS OWN NARRATIVE ARC.** I've read a lot of client manuscripts that try to "explain" the antagonist's actions by offering several chapters from the antagonist's POV. Unless you plan to redeem your antagonist so that he truly becomes a good, or better, person by story's end, this is not necessary.
- **DON'T REHASH THE SAME SCENES FROM DIFFERENT CHARACTERS' POVS.** Don't fall into the bad habit of writing the same scene from several characters' viewpoints. Unless each rendition offers new and potent plot information, you run the risk of boring readers and slowing the pace of the narrative.
- **DON'T USE NEW CHARACTERS TO OFFER NARRATIVE "INFO DUMPS" OR EXPLANATORY PLOT INFORMATION YOUR PROTAGONIST DOESN'T PROVIDE.** A viewpoint character has to exist for his own story purpose, not just to offer up key plot explanations to carry your protagonist to the next stage of the journey.
- **DON'T ADD CHARACTERS TO CREATE NEW SUBPLOTS.** Some writers feel that the best way to create a compelling plot is to include lots of subplots linked to more characters. More often than not, this leads to complications. The best plots arise from one character's problem, past wound, or current challenge. Subplots must also rise organically, like spokes radiating from a central hub rather than a tangled web of overlapping and confusing stories.
- **THE CHARACTER ARC OF EACH CO-PROTAGONIST SHOULD BE DISTINCT.** New characters are exciting and fun to write, and it's

easy to dream up a team. But it's a lot harder to develop a unique story arc for each character. If you can't quickly think of how each character not only will play an integral part in your plot but also will experience a story-worthy transformation, you're better off sticking with one protagonist.

DISTINGUISHING MULTIPLE CHARACTERS

To figure out how many co-protagonists to include in your story, analyze novels in your genre with multiple viewpoints. You'll find that three is the average number of co-protagonists, but it's by no means the rule; many novels have only two POVs. And while focusing on the struggles of more than three POV characters can cause readers to feel torn or confused, that's not to say it can't be done: Marlon James's Man Booker award–winning novel, *A Brief History of Seven Killings*, has no fewer than thirteen protagonists spanning seven hundred pages. He pulls this off by putting the viewpoint character's name at the top of each chapter so readers have no doubt whose POV they're in, and he imbues each character with a distinct voice. However, I prefer books in which readers can tell who the POV character is by his distinct voice and personality alone.

To determine how often to switch to a different viewpoint character, many writers use a formula wherein each co-protagonist gets a POV chapter or scene in a set rotating order: Protagonist A, Protagonist B, Protagonist C, all the way through the novel. Others might structure their scenes so one character appears more often than the others: A, B, A, C, A, B, A, C, or even A, A, B, C, A, A, B, C. This is where scene trackers and plot outlines come in handy. When you're juggling multiple protagonists, you will need more structural guidance to keep track of the arc and plot outcome for each one.

DETERMINING THE POV FOR EACH VIEWPOINT CHARACTER

So now let's address a crucial question: Which POV should each co-protagonist use? Should they all be in third-person intimate or all in first? Should you mix it up? Remember that when you invoke the pronoun *I* for first person, you'll need to give very strong clues each time you switch characters to identify who is speaking, otherwise many different chapters or scenes using *I* might sound similar and confuse the reader.

I've seen books that use a mix of first and third person, or first and second person. It's also common to use third-person intimate throughout, but there is no set rule. If you have three co-protagonists and one is a very deep, quiet, internal character, you may find first person most effective because it allows readers to be as intimate as possible with her. When deciding on POVs for each of your protagonists, weigh the issue of intimacy once more. If one of your protagonists feels more like the true hero of the story, or has slightly greater story responsibilities, then you may choose to put that character in an intimate POV. No simple answer exists, but only the question: How close do you want readers to get to each character's experience?

EXAMPLES OF MULTIPLE VIEWPOINTS

With so many considerations for using multiple viewpoints, it's no wonder that novelists have handled them in a variety of ways. In *The Hours* by Michael Cunningham, which pays homage to the author Virginia Woolf, the POV is mostly third-person intimate with a curious bit of omniscience tossed in here and there. In the following passages, omniscience is used to inform the reader of the time and place. Notice how the beginning of each co-protagonist's story plays upon the other, like a series of overlapping, concentric circles. Yet each character is also distinctly herself:

1. Mrs. Dalloway. Clarissa

There are still the flowers to buy. Clarissa feigns exasperation (though she loves doing errands like this), leaves Sally cleaning the bathroom, and runs out, promising to be back in half an hour.

It is New York City. It is the end of the Twentieth Century.

The vestibule door opens onto a June morning so fine and scrubbed Clarissa pauses at the threshold as she would at the edge of a pool, watching the turquoise water lapping at the tiles, the liquid nets of sun wavering in the blue depths.

2. Mrs. Woolf. Virginia

Mrs. Dalloway said something (what?), and got the flowers herself.

It is a suburb of London. It is 1923.

Virginia awakens. This might be another way to begin, certainly; with Clarissa going on an errand on a day in June, instead of soldiers marching off to lay the wreath in Whitehall. But is it the right beginning? Is it a little too ordinary? Virginia lies quietly in her bed, and sleep takes her again so quickly she is not conscious of falling back to sleep at all. It seems, suddenly, that she is not in her bed but in a park; a park impossibly verdant, green beyond green—a Platonic vision of a park, at once homely and the seat of mystery ...

3. Mrs. Brown. Lauren

Mrs. Dalloway said she would buy the flowers herself.

For Lucy had her work cut out for her. The doors would have to be taken off their hinges; Rumpelmayer's men were coming. And then, thought Clarissa Dalloway, what a morning—fresh as if issued to children on a beach.

It is Los Angeles. It is 1949.

Laura Brown is trying to lose herself. No, that's not it exactly—she is trying to keep herself by gaining entry into a parallel world.

She lays the book face down on her chest. Already her bedroom (no, their bedroom) feels more densely inhabited, more actual because a character named Mrs. Dalloway is on her way to buy flowers.

The introductions of three characters are narrated in a mix of omniscient and third-person intimate, which works well because the author is presenting three different time periods and three strong female characters with unique (though related) personal stories. The omniscient allows the author to drift through time, offering details that overlap and weave the stories together, and the intimate perspective helps us dive deeply into each woman's personal story.

Barbara Kingsolver's tour de force novel, *The Poisonwood Bible*, follows a Midwestern American family that travels to the Belgian Congo in 1959 on a religious mission and is irrevocably changed by the experience. Kingsolver uses the device of naming the character at the top of the chapter, which is especially necessary since each character is narrated in first person. Only the beautifully rendered prologue appears in the omniscient. Notice in each snippet how we get a feel for the different personalities and perspectives of each character.

Prologue

Away down below now, single file on the path, comes a woman with four girls in tow, all of them in shirtwaist dresses. Seen from above this way they are pale, doomed blossoms, bound to appeal to your sympathies. Be careful. Later on you'll have to decide what sympathy they deserve. The mother especially—watch how she leads them on, pale-eyed, deliberate. Her dark hair is tied in a ragged lace handkerchief, and her curved jawbone is lit with large false-pearl earrings, as if these headlamps from another world might show the way.

Leah Price

We came from Bethlehem, Georgia bearing Betty Crocker cake mixes into the jungle. My sisters and I were all counting on having one birthday apiece during our twelve-month mission. "And heaven knows," our mother predicted, "they won't have Betty Crocker in the Congo."

Ruth May Price

Our village is going to have this many white people: me, Rachel, Leah, and Adah. Mama. Father. That is six people. Rachel is oldest. I am youngest. Leah and Adah are in between and they're twins, so maybe they are one person, but I think two, because Leah runs everywhere and climbs trees, but Adah can't, she is bad on one whole side and doesn't talk because she is brain-damaged and also hates us all. She reads books upside down. You are only supposed to hate the Devil, and love everybody else.

Adah Price

Sunrise tantalize, evil eyes hypnotize: that is the morning, Congo pink. Any morning, every morning. Blossomy rose-color bird-song air streaked sour with breakfast cookfires. A wide red plank of dirt—the so-called road—flat-out in front of us, continuous in theory from here to somewhere distant. But the way I see it through my Adah eyes it is a flat plank clipped into pieces, rectangles and trapezoids, by the skinny black-line shadows of tall palm trunks. Through Adah eyes, oh the world is a-boggle with colors and shapes competing for a half-brain's attention.

Rachel

On Congo Easter Sunday there were no new clothes for the Price girls, that's for sure. We tromped off to church in the same old shoes and dresses we'd worn all the other African Sundays so far. No white gloves, it goes without saying. And no primping, because the only mirror we have in the house is my faux-ivory hand mirror brought from home, which we all have to share. Mother set it on the desk in the living room, propped against the wall, and every time Mama Tataba walks by it she yelps like a snake bit her. So: Easter Sunday in dirt-stained saddle oxfords, charmed I'm sure.

Orleanna Price

I could have been a different mother, you'll say. Could have straightened up and seen what was coming, for it was thick in the air all around us. It was the very odor of market day in Kilanga. Every fifth day was market day—not the seventh or thirtieth, nothing you could give a name like "Saturday" or "The First of the Month," but every thumb if you kept the days in your hand. It makes no sense at all, and then finally all the sense in the world, once you understand that keeping things in your hand is exactly how it's done in the Congo.

That Kingsolver chooses to give each sister, and their mother, her own POV is remarkable, because it broadens the scope of what could have been a small family saga—it lets the reader see the rippling effects of change and trauma within a family, and how these issues manifest differently in different characters.

In Myfanwy Collins's literary thriller *Echolocation*, in which the lives of three characters intersect in a way that will change them all forever, the author doesn't signify who is speaking at the top of the chapter, but each scene quickly and obviously establishes the POV we're in:

When the slip of the saw through trunk was buttery, liquid and verging on gentle, Geneva was moved to tears. Her body felt as though it were cutting through the tree: the rings, the history of droughts and hailstorms, the sap that could have been her own blood, dripping, weeping at her feet. It felt like a betrayal, this taking of saw to tree. But Clint was out of work again. They needed money.

Cheri rounded the final corner at the coffee shop and noted that the light cast on the brick apartment buildings recalled the light on the brick wall behind the bowling alley when she was a kid. Back where she and Geneva would hang to smoke a joint and drinks some beers before going to the school gym for roller-skating on a Friday night. The sight of it made her want to wing around and around, weaving in and out of the lines on the basketball court. She and Geneva, cracking the whip, laughing so hard they thought they would pee.

Renee felt the coming rush of customers like Harley motors thrumming down the highway. It was 4:30 when she and Rick took over from the early shift at Titty's Bar and Grille and got ready for the long night ahead. They were partners in everything, she and Rick, and had been for going on two years, which is why Jimmy Titty wanted the two of them behind the bar of his establishment. "Y'all've got my back," he said on more than one occasion. "I know y'all do." And sure they did, but that didn't mean that every once in a while some cash didn't get slipped into a pocket instead of a register or that a bottle of beer didn't get opened and drunk and never paid for.

What I love about Collins's writing is the way small details convey big character differences. Geneva is visceral and connected to her body, which makes sense, as she's physically beautiful and gets lots of attention from others for her appearance. She's also a can-do, no-nonsense type of person, which plays into the dynamic that will unfold between her and Cheri. Cheri is melancholy and emotional; she remembers specific moments in time and fixates on small details, which also plays into the plot. Renee gives people the benefit of the doubt long after it's unwise to do so, which causes her downfall. Each character leaps off the page as unique, and their distinct characterizations affect not just their voices but how the plot events of the story unfold.

NOW YOU

CHART THE ARCS

If you are planning, or have already written, a story with multiple protagonists, chart each of their four energetic markers. Then ask: How does each character contribute to the plot in a unique way?

INTRODUCE YOURSELVES

Write a paragraph beginning for each of your POV characters that introduces them via their voice in whatever POV you've planned to write in. Avoid having them directly tell the reader who they are, but try to communicate something about your character in one paragraph that is distinctly unique for each one.

Then swap the POV for one that is either more or less intimate based on what you've chosen. For instance, if you wrote in third-person intimate, try for omniscience. If you wrote in omniscient or third person, try for first or even second person, and see if it changes how your characters leap off the page.

14

SHATTERING POINT OF VIEW
Moving Beyond Traditional Forms

"In many ways, experimental writing (on the page and in other mediums) marries literature and the interactivity of theater. ... By fracturing the expected norm, you are inviting the reader to interact with his/her reading history, evaluate perceptions of life, and sometimes even to finish a story or complete an image."

—SEQUOIA NAGAMATSU

I believe that all writers should learn the basic rules of their craft before attempting to break them. In fact, this book came into being because I realized, through teaching POV, how confused many writers are about which viewpoint they're using. However, once you can tell the differences between intimate and omniscient POVs, can distinguish between internal and external vantages, and can move smoothly between different POVs from chapter to chapter, you may be ready to part with the traditional altogether. To explore the boundaries of POV, we'll look at some phenomenal examples from writers who twist and tweak POV and story structure outside of its traditional forms to create evocative, haunting, and poetic narratives; then we'll isolate what works.

THE CHORUS OR FIRST-PERSON PLURAL POINT OF VIEW

In famous Greek plays, such as the three linked plays of Sophocles's *The Oedipus Cycle*, playwrights commonly used a device known as "the chorus"—a group of people who represented the general population within the context of a particular story, often as a counterpoint to the heroes, gods, or goddesses. The chorus was comprised of multiple people who spoke as one voice and offered commentary on the events of the play, as though speaking the opinions of the audience. In some ways you might compare the chorus voice in these plays to the omniscient narrator we discussed in chapter nine, which is not so much a person as a library of knowledge that knows more than the characters do.

While you'll rarely see the chorus used in contemporary fiction, several novels employ the *we* voice, also known as the first-person plural, in which the protagonist is not one character but several, grouped together as though they share one mind, or as though one is the designated leader of the pack.

My favorite example of this POV is in Jeffrey Eugenides's novel *The Virgin Suicides*, a darkly poignant, though ultimately tragic, novel about the trials of adolescence, the burdens of growing up, and young love. It's narrated by a chorus of boys who are half in love and half fascinated with the five Lisbon girls. The sisters—Cecilia, Lux, Bonnie, Mary, and Therese—range in age from thirteen to seventeen, and all meet their end in suicide. We are introduced to the girls through the chorus POV:

> [The Lisbon sisters] were short, round-buttocked in denim with roundish cheeks that recalled that same dorsal softness. Whenever we got a glimpse, their faces looked indecently revealed, as though we were used to seeing women in veils.

Here, *we* is synonymous with *I*.

Later the group of boys interacts with the sisters at a party hosted by the Lisbon parents after Cecilia unsuccessfully tries to commit suicide:

> The party was just beginning to get fun when Cecilia slipped off her stool and made her way to her mother. Playing with the bracelets on her left wrist, she asked if she could be excused. It was the only time we ever heard her speak, and we were surprised by the maturity of her voice. More than anything she sounded old and tired. She kept pulling on the bracelets, until Mrs. Lisbon said, "If that's what you want, Cecilia. But we've gone to all this trouble to have a party for you."

So why opt to form a chorus instead of a main character? By grouping the boys into a pack, the sisters remain the protagonists, and thus the focus, of the story. The boys are simply the observational unit that tell the story of the sisters to the reader. And perhaps Eugenides felt that these sisters should come across as so magnetic they could command the attention of not just one boy but an entire posse. Whatever the reason, in a rather brilliant way, the author has created an omniscient narrator who possesses the intimacy of a first-person narrator.

Plus, by never entering the sisters' POV directly, Eugenides keeps a powerful tension alive. Both the readers and the chorus don't know what is happening in this family to drive five beautiful young girls to attempt suicide. If the author chose to enter the sisters' POV, that mystery would be quickly dissolved—they would have told us themselves, eliminating the need to ask questions.

Another example of the chorus POV can be found in Eleanor Brown's literary novel *The Weird Sisters*. The title is taken from a Shakespearean play, and the story is tightly woven, thematically, around Shakespearean drama. The three very different Andreas sisters were raised by a father who is a professor of Shakespeare, and who communicates almost exclusively in verse. The sisters are also named after the three daughters of King Lear: Rose (Rosalind), Bean (Bianca), and Cordy (Cordelia).

When Cordy, the nomadic sister who has never stayed long in one place or had a reliable job, suspects she is pregnant, the scene is narrated by the chorus of her sisters:

> She yanked open the box, tossing the instructions in the direction of the trash can, and did the deed. Huddled on the toilet in the bathroom, tile cracked and shedding beneath her feet, staring at the pink line, pale as fading newsprint, her conscience caught up with her.
>
> "It doesn't get much lower than this, old Cordy, old sock," she could hear Bean telling her cheerfully.
>
> "How are you going to take care of a baby if you can't even afford a pregnancy test?" Rose harped.
>
> Cordy brushed our imaginary voices aside and buried the evidence in the trash can. It didn't make a difference, really, she told herself.

Each sister gets her turn to be the focus of a chapter, but the narrator is always the sisterly chorus.

Again, we ask the question: Why the chorus POV? What purpose does it serve? First, this book plays homage to Shakespearean plays by adopting a poetic tone and addressing issues of family and loyalty, the intertwining ropes of fate, and the lifelong consequences of one bad choice. By weaving the POVs of the three sisters together, the theme of family, of being bound to each other, is firmly reinforced. It also creates a poetic quality that echoes the work of Shakespeare himself.

Omniscient and chorus POVs can feel dreamlike or epic—their widened scope allows for a vaster body of influence, impressions, and information from which the writer can draw.

Another reason a writer might take on this POV is simply to try something different. Writing doesn't always have to cater to the familiar; many writers like to play, experiment, and push boundaries and expectations.

When using the chorus POV, take the following into consideration:

- **TONE:** Will your chorus voice have a wry, witty tone or a somber, serious one? Stay consistent.
- **THEME:** Chorus POV works well when it's tied to the theme of a story. If yours spans history, or touches upon mythology, or includes an element of fantasy or the paranormal, you have more leeway to play with a chorus.
- **IDENTITY:** Though your chorus will include multiple people, it helps to imagine it as a singular entity, with a style that sounds the same each time it makes an appearance. You might try and imagine it as one person with several personalities, or as a group of people that must follow a certain set of rules.

FRACTURED NARRATIVES

Another way to play with POV lies in the realm of the fractured narrative, in which you can disassemble the narrative structure and piece together memories, scenes, or events to form a cohesive whole or work within a limited framework. These novels offer entry into characters and themes that may be difficult to achieve through traditional forms and narrative structures.

In S.J. Watson's thriller *Before I Go to Sleep,* the protagonist is a woman with amnesia who finds a diary every day when she wakes with notes and information compiled by herself and her husband that fill in the bits and pieces of her memory. The reader knows only as much as she knows, and there are more questions than answers:

I stare for a moment, then wriggle my fingers. The fingers of the hand holding the soap move also. I gasp, and the soap thuds into the sink. I look up at the mirror.

The face I see looking back at me is not my own. The hair has no volume and is cut much shorter than I wear it; the skin on the cheeks and under the chin sags; the lips are thin; the mouth turned down. I cry out, a wordless gasp that would turn into a shriek of shock were I to let it, and then notice the eyes. The skin around them is lined, yes, but despite everything else, I can see that they are mine. The person in the mirror is me, but I am twenty years too old. Twenty-five. More.

This isn't possible. I begin to shake and grip the edge of the sink. Another scream begins to rise in my chest and this one erupts as a strangled gasp. I step back, away from the mirror, and it is then that I see them. Photographs. Taped to the wall, to the mirror itself. Pictures, interspersed with yellow pieces of gummed paper, felt-tipped notes, damp and curling.

I choose one at random. *Christine*, it says, and an arrow points to a photograph of me—this new me, this old me—in which I am sitting on a bench on the side of a quay, next to a man. The name seems familiar, but only distantly so, as if I am having to make an effort to believe that it is mine. In the photograph we are both smiling at the camera, holding hands. He is handsome, attractive, and when I look closely, I can see that it is the same man I slept with, the one I left in the bed. The word *Ben* is written beneath it, and next to it, *Your husband*.

Here, the author is working within Christine's fractured, limited memory, and we must rely on the clues and cues provided to her, just as she does. It's an interesting way to play with POV as well: It differs from typical first person because the reader can't trust that the protagonist knows what is happening or that she is reliable. It creates a wonderfully awful page-turning tension.

Jenny Offill's novel *Dept. of Speculation* is another fractured narrative: a novel told in fragments, vignettes, lines of poetry, scientific facts, and personal anecdotes woven together into a story. It's evocative and emotional, and, like other fractured narratives, it evokes powerful feelings in lieu of a linear story. The paragraphs are even structured with space between them as though each one could be plucked off the page and rearranged to the reader's liking, like a puzzle or collage:

> Researchers looked at magnetic resonance images of the brains of people who described themselves as newly in love. They were shown a photograph of their beloveds while their brains were scanned for activity. The scan showed the same reward systems being activated as in the brains of addicts given a drug.
>
> *Ca-ching! Ca-ching! Ca-ching!*
>
> For most married people, the standard pattern is a decrease of passionate love, but an increase in deep attachment. It is thought that this attachment response evolved in order to keep partners together long enough to have and raise children. Most mammals don't raise their offspring together, but humans do.
>
> There is nowhere to cry in this city. But the wife has an idea one day. There is a cemetery half a mile from their apartment. Perhaps one could wander through it sobbing without unnerving anyone. Perhaps one could flap one's hands even.

Offill creates an omniscient-feeling voice out of this mosaic of limited third-person POV of "the wife" and these bits of patchwork information. Strangely, it adds up to the feeling of a very wise narrator who both imparts wisdom beyond the main character's perspective and yet sympathizes with her experiences. It's a wonderful blend of both.

However, my most favorite example of a contemporary fractured narrative is Lidia Yuknavitch's novel *The Small Backs of Children*. It is as much a novel of ideas and feelings as it is a specific plot happening to specific characters. Yuknavitch consciously eschews much of typical novel structure for something much different. She spoke about her choices in a July 2015 interview with *Fiction Advocate* magazine:

> I made formal choices the way that I did because the traditional formal choices available to me didn't seem adequate for the story

Writing the Intimate Character

I wanted to tell. I didn't want to write a book based on psychological realism. Nor one based on genre or fantasy nor historical fiction. I wanted to write a new kind of novel, where the formal play in the book connects to the corporeal and emotional experiences of women and girls. To do that, I had to abandon everything I've learned about literary traditions and reinvent story.

In place of stable individual characters, I created temporary and fragmented subjectivities. In this case their names became deprioritized while the state they are in at any given moment is amplified.

In place of character development I asserted emotional intensities—glimpses of people and things juxtaposed over time, sometimes in order, sometimes not, because that's how we experience things—in pieces, not lines.

In place of linear plot I wove multiple story threads that braid or unravel or repeat or dissolve. I let form loose.

In place of a beginning that holds still and an ending that is stable and resolves things, I opted for something more like life— parallel possibilities that fracture and disperse between readers.

Her characters don't have names but rather are identified by simple nouns: "The Girl," the war-ravaged ostensible protagonist of the novel who remakes herself from the wreckage of loss and rape through art; "The Writer," who is so affected by a photo of The Girl that she sinks into a depression where she cannot write; "The Poet;" "The Photographer," and so on. The Girl and The Writer might be considered co-protagonists, for it is The Girl's trauma that drives The Writer's fate in this story. Yuknavitch shifts POV, too, from chapter to chapter. The Girl is narrated in omniscient that moves from her intimate, internal vantage to the external, distant, all-knowing voice. In contrast, The Writer is narrated in first person. Some scenes are written in the form of a play, others in lines of prose poetry. Some chapters contain only a single sentence.

Just as Yuknavitch intended, the book feels like a set of experiences rather than a linear story, which conveys the themes she wanted to plant in the minds of readers. While this won't work for every story—or even many—it works very well for stories with themes of trauma and violence that reflect the way people retain memories of and experience tragedy.

In a fractured narrative, you don't have to worry about staying as rigidly true to a POV in the same way as with a traditional or linear character structure. That's not to say you can fly without any guidelines, but you do have room to play.

When writing a fractured narrative, consider the following:

- **WRITE WHOLE FIRST.** Rather than trying to write in fragments, consider writing a linear narrative and then breaking it apart to reflect the journey your characters must go through.
- **UNIVERSALIZE.** Consider making your character more of an archetype than an individual person. Is your character defined by her trade, or by his experience? Is he perhaps The War Veteran instead of a young Marine from the South? Is she perhaps The Singer rather than a struggling young performer from a family who doesn't value the arts? Think of ways to make your character represent a universal condition or issue rather than focusing on all the little details that make a character so unique.
- **ADVANCE THE STORY.** Even if you break a narrative into pieces, each piece must still advance the story and the characters in some way. We must learn something new in each scene and see character change by the end.
- **PROVIDE PURPOSE.** Choose to write a fragmented story only if you have a purpose in mind. Trauma, amnesia, accidents, war, abuse—these are all situations that might offer themselves to a nonlinear narrative. Doing it "just for fun" is fine if you enjoy experimenting with writing, but if you intend to share it with an audience, consider how the fractured narrative will still provide a story.
- **RESEARCH.** If necessary, do your research to find out how people experience the subject(s) you plan to write in this way. If your character struggles with memory loss or grief, do some research so you can render the experience realistically.

Writing the Intimate Character

LYRICAL FORMS

Since poetry has a way of bypassing the intellect and going straight to the gut through symbolic language and unique juxtaposition, some writers choose to drift out of linear, straightforward language and into the poetic realm. Poetry feels very intimate, as though it is the language of our collective unconscious. So even if you choose to write in a distant, external POV, if you're relying heavily on lyrical forms, you're likely to achieve an intimate feeling, as if you were writing in a limited, intimate POV.

Matt Bell's novel *In the House upon the Dirt Between the Lake and the Woods* is, on the surface, a story about a couple that experiences and copes with a miscarriage. But Bell opts to tell the story almost as if it is a creation myth from an ancient culture. He leans heavily on symbols, dreamlike schisms of reality, and nonliteral translations of events. The novel is like one big metaphor. And yet, strangely, it works. Here are a couple of scenes that show the way he uses metaphor and how he departs from linear structure:

> Only then did my wife stand in the rowboat, her movements sudden, unannounced. I worked to steady the boat and so did not grasp her intent when she began to sing, for the first time using her voice not to create or cast up shapes but to take them down—and how could I have even hoped to stop such a power?
>
> With song after song, with a song for each of their names, my wife lured some number of the stars one by one from out the sky, and those so named could not resist her call. Their lights dropped and crashed all around us, nearly upon us, and though they dimmed as they fell, still they landed too bright for our smaller world, and I shielded my face against the flash of their collisions, then covered my ears against the booming that followed.

This is one of the first passages following the wife's miscarriage, and it is lyrically evocative of how a man might feel in the face of the loss of their child: that his wife is both extremely powerful, having created and then lost a life in her own body, and a creature beyond his understanding who possesses the power to create and destroy life. The style of the writing is rhythmic and mythic, more creation myth than novel.

Later in the novel, his wife has left him after he rejected her changeling child, a bear cub passing as a human whom she claims is their son. He has gone to live in the depths of a cave beneath what was once their home. When he returns to reclaim and reconnect with her, he drops into poetic language as he enters room after room:

> And in this room, a silence that had once been a song.
> And in this room, a light that had once been lightning.
> And in this room, a heat that had once been a fire.
> And in this room, a lump of silver that had once been a ring, two rings.
> And in this room, the taste of burned hair. And in this room, its smell.
> And in this room, the carapace of bees, long ago emptied.
> And in this room, a wine bottle, full of the leavings of maggots but not maggots.
> And in this room, a broken bowl of mirrors, reflecting nothing.

Each of these "rooms" is likely a memory, a metaphor of some other time in the couple's lives when they were happy or in a different state from where they are now. And while none of it is logical or literal, it evokes powerful emotion. And each image is powerfully intimate, evocative of the limited POVs.

Leza Lowitz's young adult novel *Up from the Sea* is a story told completely in poetic verse. It's set in the aftermath of the 9.0 earthquake that struck Japan in 2011 and the ensuing tsunami that destroyed entire villages. I believe that Lowitz chose poetry to tell this story because it is so difficult to capture the magnitude of great trauma in literal verse. As Lidia Yuknavitch says in talking about why she structured her novel the way she did, we don't experience trauma in fully rendered memories or in pictures brimming with detail; we recount it in disembodied slivers and pieces.

Here is an excerpt from *Up from the Sea*:

HEART POUNDING
legs pounding
head pounding
obstacle course of
crumbled buildings
chunks of pavement
rooftops strewn like train tracks
tracks buckled like busted rooftops
downed electric cables
splintered boards
upturned cars
ships on land
flattened trucks.

Each block
is like
a continent
to cross.

BLACK MONSTER
raging,
smashing
into land,
exploding
in sky-high spray
snapping
crunching
crushing
everything
in its wake.

Horns beeping
cars swirling
water
sweeping up
busesstreetlampsshopsigns
homesbuildingtrees
even people.

The line breaks of the poetic form also bypass the intellect and go straight for the heart and gut, which creates instant intimacy and an immediacy that makes the reader feel as though she is actually experiencing these unforgettable moments.

Fractured and lyrical narratives are powerful and memorable. They remain lodged in the minds and hearts of readers long after they finish the last page. These stories are, of course, hard to write well, so be patient with yourself if your first draft isn't entirely successful. Sometimes stories of this nature take several drafts to fully form.

NOW YOU

CREATE YOUR OWN CHORUS

Imagine adding a chorus POV to your current project or one you plan to write. Answer the following questions:

- Who might this group of voices be?
- What do they have to say?
- Why are they together?
- What observations do they bring to your novel that an individual character can't?

Attempt to write a scene in the chorus POV where the chorus oversees or overhears something another character believes he is doing in secret.

Write another scene where the chorus encounters something shocking or upsetting.

Now rewrite the chorus scenes in your chosen POV. Notice the differences between the POVs. Which one feels more organic to the story you're telling?

FRACTURE THE WHOLE

Select four key plot points or scenes in your novel or story, perhaps the four energetic markers of your plot, and rewrite them in *only* sensory imagery and internal monologue, without real-time action or dialogue. In essence, you get carte blanche not to "show." See how much information you can convey when you go completely internal. Now, write these scenes again without sensory imagery, using only action and dialogue. See if something new emerges or if these scenes create an interesting structure all their own.

UNLEASH THE LYRICAL

Choose a linear, traditional scene from your existing work and recast it as a poem, like the excerpts from Matt Bell's or Leza Lowitz's novels. What is the emotional truth of the scene? What images or metaphors can you use to conjure the same essential feelings? Can you employ alliteration or short sentence fragments? Try to pull out the images, if any have emerged. If you want to write something from scratch, imagine a character in her Dark Night, in which she has just experienced a terrible crisis, loss, or death. Now try to tell that story in poetic form.

15

LITERARY DEVICES
In Lieu of Point of View

"Literature adds to reality, it does not simply describe it. It enriches the necessary competencies that daily life requires and provides; and in this respect, it irrigates the deserts that our lives have already become."

—C.S. LEWIS

We all prefer to read and write certain types of stories. Personally I prefer stories filtered directly through one character's POV at a time. However, I accept that we now live in digital times and experience reality differently as a result of new and changing media. Our literature ought to reflect this shift. This chapter will look at the various literary devices that offer alternative methods to communicate plot and character information not filtered through traditional character POV. We will also explore how to render these devices actively and avoid the trap of dull narrative summary.

A caveat before we begin: Just like too much internal monologue, too many literary devices can eventually stagnate your story, slow down the pace, and feel like lazy storytelling, so be judicious and strategic.

BOOKS WITHIN BOOKS

Harry Potter fans will be familiar with several books that Hermione, one of Harry's best friends at their wizarding school, Hogwarts, regularly pulls information from and chides Harry and Ron for not reading. Some of these wonderful fictional books include *Fantastic Beasts and Where to Find Them* by Newt Scamander, *The Standard Book of Spells* by Miranda Goshawk, or the series written by the self-important Gilderoy Lockhart, with titles like *Gadding with Ghouls* and *Voyages with Vampires*. These books serve several functions, though the reader never gets the chance to read any of them in full. A book within a book might also be useful to your story.

Sources of Information

These books can act as sources of information your characters can draw from, eliminating the need to enter omniscient POV. Hermione, the lovable know-it-all, constantly quotes from books she has studied because she is a voracious reader and it's true to her character, but having her do so also relieves the author from calling on omniscience to convey the same information. This method is much more active. However, take caution: To make these books within books believable, you need to have more than a passing idea of what they contain. You may even have to write portions of them to authentically convey the information within.

Worldbuilding

These books are another part of what makes the universe of Harry Potter so realistic—no details have been overlooked, and an entire canon of literature exists to back up every strange and magical element in this universe.

Many writers, particularly those who write fantasy, write notebooks full of details about the world their story is set in and its history and customs. Even if you use only a fraction of this information in the actual story, it has a way of seeping through the cracks and creating authenticity and depth that your story might not have otherwise.

Character Development

In Rainbow Rowell's YA novel *Fangirl*, Cather "Cath" Avery, who is about to begin her first year of college, is deeply immersed in reading and writing fan fiction based on a series of fantasy novels about a mage named Simon Snow. The book bounces between her third-person intimate POV and sections of Simon Snow books written in omniscient. Here's Cath's POV in one scene, which shows us her direct experience:

> Cath imagined herself at her laptop. She tried to put into words how it felt, what happened when it was good, when it was working, when the words were coming out of her before she knew what they were, bubbling up from her chest, like rhyming, like rapping, *like jump-roping*, she thought, jumping just before the rope hits your ankles.
>
> "To share something true," another girl said. Another pair of RayBans.
>
> Cath shook her head.
>
> "Why do we write fiction?" Professor Piper asked.
>
> Cath looked down at her notebook.
>
> *To disappear.*

The next scene is a page from the book within a book, *Simon Snow and the Mage's Heir*:

> He was so focused—and frustrated—he didn't even see the girl with the red hair sit down at his table. She had pigtails and old-fashioned pointy spectacles, the kind you'd wear to a fancy dress party if you were going as a witch.
>
> "You're just going to tire yourself out," the girl said.
>
> "I'm just trying to do this right," Simon grunted, tapping the two-pence coin again with his wand and furrowing his brow painfully. Nothing happened.
>
> "Here," she said, crisply waving her hand over the coin.
>
> She didn't have a wand, but she wore a large purple ring. There was yarn wound round it to keep it on her finger. *"Fly away home."*
>
> With a shiver, the coin grew six legs and a thorax and started to scuttle away. The girl swept it gently off the desk into a jar.
>
> "How did you do that?" Simon asked.

Rowell juxtaposes scenes from the fictional Simon Snow books with key moments in Cath's story, using them to provide depth and context and to parallel Cath's own inner journey, as she faces off with the fact that adolescence is coming to an end and that her twin sister doesn't want to room with her in college.

The end of the book contains an excerpt of a story written by Cath and published in *Prairie Schooner*, a respected literary journal:

> The problem with playing hide-and-seek with your sister is that sometimes she gets bored and stops looking for you.
>
> And there you are—under the couch, in the closet, wedged behind the lilac tree—and you don't want to give up, because maybe she's just biding her time. But maybe she's wandered off. …
>
> You wait. You wait until you forget that you're waiting, until you forget that there's anything to you beyond stillness and quiet; an ant crawls over your knee, and you don't flinch. And it doesn't matter now whether she's coming for you—the hiding is enough.

The excerpt shows that Cath has grown into the writer she wanted to be, despite having written fan fiction, which others sneered at and didn't consider "real writing." It also demonstrates that she now understands that she and her sister are separate people who must learn to live separate lives.

Backstory

Another example of the books-within-books device comes from Lev Grossman's Magicians trilogy. Quentin Coldwater grew up reading a series of books by a writer named Christopher Plover, about a fantastical land called Fillory, which a family of young siblings discovers in the back of their bedroom closet. (Plover's books are clearly patterned after C.S. Lewis's Narnia series.) When Quentin graduates high school, he learns that he is a magician and that Fillory is real—and just like the fictional kids who went there in the books by Plover, Quentin and his school friends end up there as well.

Grossman uses the Fillory books as a wonderful way to report backstory: The characters often compare what they have read to the reality they encounter. This technique is a shortcut for the author to offer information that might otherwise have required considerably more time and longer scenes, and it also helps develop character. For what is growing up if not facing the fact that adult reality is never quite what you imagined as a child?

> Quentin hadn't always been a king, of Fillory or anywhere else. None of them had. Quentin had grown up a regular non-magical, non-royal person in Brooklyn, in what he still in spite of everything thought of as the real world. He'd thought Fillory was fiction, an enchanted land that existed only as the setting of a series of fantasy novels for children. But then he'd learned to do magic, at a secret college called Brakebills, and he and his friends had found out that Fillory was real.
>
> It wasn't what they expected. Fillory was a darker and more dangerous place in real life than it was in the books. Bad things happened there, terrible things. People got hurt and killed and worse. Quentin went back to Earth in disgrace and despair. His hair turned white.

Now, if you're about to say, "Hey, that's all backstory info dump, not a scene," you're technically right—this paragraph appears early in Book Two of the series and serves as a quick overview to orient readers to what happened in Book One, eliminating the need for a ton of flashbacks. Grossman includes very few of these synopses—almost all of the story is written in scenes—but this excerpt gives you a feel for the way he uses books within books to compare the characters' expectations to reality.

TECHNOLOGY AS A STORYTELLING DEVICE

We live in a digital age, in which people communicate as much, if not more, through electronic means than in person. Contemporary literature has incorporated different kinds of media, from texts and instant messages to social media platforms, audio recordings, and e-mails, because these digital communiqués are now a way of life for most people under forty. As someone born before the Internet, and who was a latecomer to social media like Facebook and Twitter, I confess it took me some time to get used to reading about these forms of media in contemporary fiction, much less stories composed *in* these forms. Yet this is our reality: Younger people text, tweet, Snapchat, and make Vine videos. They communicate via Instagram and new methods I'm sure I know nothing about. Not only does including these devices convey authenticity, if you're writing contemporary fiction you're required to include it, or at least mention it, to create a realistic setting. The really cool thing about it all is that it opens up new storytelling doors.

Texts and Tweets

YA author Lauren Myracle was among the first authors to embrace digital storytelling with her book *ttyl* (digital shorthand for "talk to you later"). All of her novels, which use instant messaging and texting as the sole medium for telling the story, have been wild successes among young readers.

Here's an example from her novel *l8r, g8r* ("later, gator"). You might find it hard to read if you're past a certain age and uncomfortable with the language of texting and messaging—but, again, it worked for younger readers. If you are writing books for an audience younger than you, it's crucial to do your research and write in a way that is authentic to their experience. Myracle clearly has her finger on the pulse:

> zoegirl: maddie!! i'm so excited, i can't sit still! i can't *believe* i'm gonna c doug in 2 hrs!
>
> **mad maddie: i hear ya—even im kinda excited to c the guy. i wonder if he's changed?**
>
> zoegirl: it's been SIX ENTIRE MONTHS. *6 months* of no doug!
>
> zoegirl: aye-yai-yai—what if he doesn't like me anymore?
>
> **mad maddie: oh, please. Doug is doug is doug, and no semester at sea is gonna change that.**
>
> **mad maddie: anyway, haven't u guys been writing like 5,000 letters a day?**
>
> zoegirl: that's true, and his letters are so sweet. that's 1 cool thing— since internet usage was "strongly discouraged" on the ship, i now have actual love letter to save for when i'm older. Sooo romantic!

These text examples have an immediacy that's a lot like first-person POV, or even the hyper-immediacy of second person.

E-mails, Memos, and Letters

Before the invention of e-mail, we had the epistolary novel—a story told in letters exchanged between characters. E-mail, of course, is the modern form of the letter, though some writers still use traditional handwritten correspondence as well. Memos—as in letters disseminated within a workplace—are another variation on the letter/e-mail often used in books. One of my favorite novels that tells a story almost exclusively in a combination of e-mails and memos is Maria Semple's darkly comic novel, *Where'd You Go, Bernadette*, about a woman who seems ill-suited to the job of PTA mom at her daughter Bee's private school, and whose complex history is revealed over the course of the book.

Bernadette tells much of her story in e-mails to her virtual assistant (VA), Manjula. Other pieces of the story are revealed in e-mails between gossipy parents at Bernadette's daughter's school, Galer Street, and a couple of transcripts from a police report.

Here's a taste of Bernadette. Ostensibly, she's writing to her VA to help her pay a bill, but in the process she reveals far too much (something she does in every e-mail):

> Attached please find a scan of an emergency room bill I suppose I should pay. One of the gnats at Galer Street claims I ran over her foot at pickup. I would laugh at the whole thing, but I'm too bored. See that's why I call the mothers there "gnats." Because they're annoying, but not so annoying that you actually want to spend valuable energy on them. These gnats have done everything to provoke me into a fight over the past nine years—the stories I could tell! Now that Bee is graduating and I can smell the barn, it's not worth waging a gnat battle over. Could you check our various insurance policies to see if something covers it?

And here's an example of a letter Bernadette sends to an old work colleague in her former life. This exchange beautifully captures her voice and her personality and tells us a few things about her at the same time:

> Paul,
> Greetings from sunny Seattle, where women are "gals," people are "folks," a little bit is a "skosh," if you're tired you're "logy," if something is slightly off it's "hinky," you can't sit Indian-style but you can sit "crisscross applesauce," when the sun comes out it's never called "sun" but always "sunshine," boyfriends and girlfriends are "partners," nobody swears but someone might occasionally "drop the f-bomb," you're allowed to cough but only into your elbow, and any request, reasonable or unreasonable, is met with, "no worries."
> Have I mentioned how much I hate it here?
> But it is the tech capital of the world, and we have this thing called "the Internet," which allows us to do something called a

"Google search," so if we run into a random guy outside the public library and he starts talking about an architecture competition in L.A. inspired by let's say, *oneself*, we can type that information into the aforementioned "Google search" and learn more.

Letters like this fall into the category of "as told to" second person and make us feel as though we are the recipients of the letter. It's relatively intimate in that we feel close to the writer of the letters, and slightly distant in that we are not identified as the writer of the letters—in this case, Bernadette.

If you're looking for a novel that really stretches the use of literary devices, read Meg Cabot's novel *Boy Meets Girl*. The author uses a vast array of devices, including posters, memos, employee incident reports, e-mails, journal entries, transcripts, voicemails, instant messages, newspaper articles, and more. In one particularly effective scene, she intersperses the character's thoughts beneath the items on a menu, a technique she repeats for several different restaurants, reflecting the character's different moods. Check out how this device injects a sense of fun and playfulness, and shows that the character is caught up in her emotional turmoil even while doing something as mundane as deciding what to eat:

LUPE'S MEXICAN CANTEENA

Appetizers

Soup of the day $3.75

Oh my God, I am so fired. I can't believe how fired I am. Why did I have to start crying during the

Guacamole $3.75

interview? Why didn't I think to turn the tape off before I started bawling my head off?

Sweet Plantains $2.75

Why can't I be like the T.O.D? SHE would never cry while firing someone. But I don't WANT to be

Yucca Fries $2.75

like the T.O.D. I hate her. I should just quit. Now I have to find a new job on top of a new apt. and

Nachos with Cheese $3.95

boyfriend. WHY IS EVERYTHING BAD HAPPENING TO ME ALL AT ONCE??? And why

Each device carries a different tone and serves a different purpose, adding a complex and, at times, quite comical feel to the story that makes for an amusing, breezy read.

Audio

Having your protagonist stumble across some form of audio recording is another method to get the voice of a character across and fill in backstory. From old-fashioned cassette tapes to modern MP3s, this device gives you a lot of latitude to play. One notable use of audio appears in Jay Asher's YA novel *Thirteen Reasons Why*, in which a boy, Clay, receives a box of cassette tapes from a classmate, Hannah, who committed suicide. At first, he wants nothing to do with these tapes, but eventually he listens, and what he hears changes him irrevocably. The lines in italics are from Hannah's audio tapes, and the other lines are Clay's internal monologue:

> *Hello, boys and girls. Hannah Baker here. Live and in stereo.*
> I don't believe it.
> *No return engagements. No encore. And this time, absolutely no requests.*
> No, I can't believe it. Hannah Baker killed herself.
> *I hope you're ready, because I'm about to tell you the story of my life. More specifically, why my life ended. And if you're listening to these tapes, you're one of the reasons why.*
> What? No!
> *I'm not saying which tape brings you into the story. But fear not, if you received this lovely little box, your name will pop up …
> I promise.*

This is just one of many ways you can bring in the voice or viewpoint of a character who can't speak for herself and provide backstory or information that takes place outside the time line of the novel. However, remember that including too much narrative, even with the use of a literary device, will slow the pace, so be sure to weave it around action, dialogue, and sensory imagery to keep the story moving.

DIARY ENTRIES

Like letters, diary or journal entries are some of the most commonly used devices in literature. They easily show the inner workings of a character, particularly to reveal information to another character. They allow room for conflict—for instance, a character could read someone else's diary and learn a troubling secret, or the diary could act as a confessional after a major plot event, revealing information the character never revealed in person. I recommend against using too many diary entries in a novel unless they are written in active and sensory scenes.

Ruth Ozeki's novel *A Tale for the Time Being* is told in two POVs: one in the first-person viewpoint of the protagonist, Ruth, a middle-aged woman who lives on a remote island in the Pacific Northwest, and another POV delivered from the diary pages of a sixteen-year-old Japanese girl named Nao that washes onto the shore near Ruth's house.

Nao's entries alternate between more passive narrative summary and active scenes. Here's an excerpt that uses the former:

> It's not really my fault that I screwed up my entrance exams. With my educational background, I couldn't get into a good Japanese school no matter how much I crammed. My dad wants me to apply to an international high school. He wants me to go to Canada. He's got this thing about Canada. He says it's like America only with health care and no guns, and you can live up to your potential there and not have to worry about what society thinks or about getting sick or getting shot.

Writing the Intimate Character

Later, Nao goes with her mother to the local baths, and a woman notices bruises on Nao's arms. Nao's entry of this event is rendered in scene:

"Oh! What happened to you, young lady? Do you have a rash?"

At first Mom didn't pay any attention, but then the old bitch actually called to her and said, "Okusan, Okusan! What is wrong with your daughter's skin? She's got butsubutsu all over her. I hope she doesn't have a disease."

Mom came and stood next to me as I hunched over my bucket. She took my wrist and raised my arm and turned it over, looking at the underside where the bruises were most dense. Her fingers dug into my wrist bones and it hurt more than when the kids at school pinched me.

"Maybe she shouldn't be going into the water," the old bitch said. "If it's a rash, it could be contagious."

My mom let my arm drop. "Tondemonai," she said. "Those are just bruises from her gym class. They were playing too roughly. Isn't that right, Naoko?"

Both excerpts are recounted in Nao's diary, but in the second excerpt, Ozeki stays as much within an active scene as possible so that the pace of the diary entries never drags.

It's up to you to decide if you want to pull from the dozens of literary devices that fall outside the purview of traditional POV to offer information, provide character backstory, and drive your plot forward.

NOW YOU

GETTING TO KNOW YOU

For each of your viewpoint characters, answer the following questions:

- How would you sum up each character in one sentence? In one word?
- What is each character's flaw? Strength?

- What is each character's story goal?
- What unique quality does each character contribute to the plot?
- How does each character's storyline intersect with the other main characters'?

16

TRY IT ON FOR SIZE
How to Pick the Right Point of View

> *"For what you see and hear depends a good deal on where you are standing: it also depends on what sort of person you are."*

—C.S. LEWIS, *THE MAGICIAN'S NEPHEW*

By reading this book you should now have a solid sense of what POV looks like, inside and out, and how to recognize and use character cues to enhance your stories. If you're now familiar with at least one POV you didn't previously know much about, even better. What follows is a series of considerations and checklists to help you determine which POV(s) will work best for your book. However, I urge you to play with the exercises in chapter seventeen as well. Even if you think you've landed on the perfect POV, you might be surprised by what happens to your story when you switch to another.

WRITING CHARACTERS WHO ARE NOT LIKE YOU

The best stories are mosaics of characters, which means that you'll likely write about people who are not like you: Your cast might represent a wide range of genders, ages, and racial and ethnic backgrounds, and they'll most certainly be caught in conflicts different from your own experiences. Heck, sometimes great characters are not even human. As writers we can act as magnificent translators of experience, even when we haven't directly shared that experience. I think writers have higher-than-usual empathy meters and a knack for observation that aid them in creating characters very different from themselves.

However, just because your character may differ from you in a variety of ways doesn't excuse you from looking deeply into your own motivations. In a blog post on writing about race in novels, author Mitali Perkins asks us to consider, when writing a character whose ethnicity differs from our own, why we've chosen to do so:

> *First*, why **are** you describing the ethnicity of your characters? Don't do it if your honest answer is "I want to show how open-minded I am" or "I want to move the world towards a better day."
>
> A better answer might be "because the particular community where the action is set is diverse." Or: "because my protagonist knows how to make kimchee from scratch."
>
> The story and characters, and not your best political intentions, should determine whether or not you provide ethnic cues in description.

She also cautions against using dialect and jargon in character speech as cop-outs for doing deeper work to convey ethnicity. All characters must feel like realized, rounded people—and that means doing deep work.

Following are a few more key elements to consider when writing characters who are not (like) you.

Empathy

Coming to the page to write about a character who isn't you and is *un*like you requires keen empathy—the ability to imagine and understand how another person might feel. It takes extra-special focus on details so that you can convey a believable character. Empathy requires understanding; I can feel sorry for someone who is having a bad experience, but only once I have imagined what it would be like in his shoes can I also empathize. (And let's be honest: You might not be able to truly understand some people's situations at a deep level.) You must also show the struggles and histories of your characters in fully realized scenes so that the reader also experiences empathy. The last thing you want is for your readers to feel only pity—or worse, scorn—for your characters. If you bring empathy into your character development process, readers will recognize and feel that empathy, too.

Cultural and Ethnic Representation

Writers have formed many different opinions about whether it is a good idea to write a character from an entirely different culture and racial identity than their own. Yet many authors have done so, and continue to do so. For example, if you wish to present fiction that exists in a diverse universe, it's important to consider that not all your characters be white men. The most important factor when writing a character of a background different from yours is adequate research. This includes talking to real people, not just flipping through books, so that you can maintain appropriate sensitivity to cultural information, terminology, and history that you may not be privy to already. This is a massive undertaking, especially if you are working with different cultural and racial identities. It's more common for writers to create characters of a different age or gender than their own, though it's still quite challenging to get them right.

Remember that details about your character's appearance and speech patterns are not enough to communicate a character of a different race, cultural background, gender, or age. You must be careful not to slip into reductive stereotypes and clichés, which are annoying at best and offensive at worst.

Accuracy

In order to be sensitive, you need to be accurate, which takes us back to the issue of research. To effectively write about a character from another culture, you need to do more than find out how she talks, dresses, and eats—you need to understand her history in the particular time period in which she lives, as well as cultural mores, politics, and customs. This goes for writing about an African-American character if you're white, or writing about citizens of Spain if you're Canadian. Don't fall prey to clichés that assume all women are emotional or all men are instinctual, or whatever beliefs you may hold. Be willing to be wrong in your assumptions about this other person, whether he or she differs from you in gender or age, or lives in a different time.

CHECKLISTS FOR PICKING THE RIGHT POV

When you're ready to choose a POV for your story, use this set of checklists as a litmus test. Keep in mind that you do not need to meet *all* the criteria in a particular POV's checklist in order to choose it. Even one or two points may be enough.

Reasons to Choose First Person

- I want to give readers as intimate a view of my character as possible.
- I want to allow my character's strong opinions and observations free reign.
- I do not need to reveal more than one character's POV at a time. (Note: You can have more than one first-person character in a novel, as long as you give each of them his or her own scenes or chapters.)

- My story works when limited to only one character's knowledge.
- My story depends on the limited scope of only one character's POV.
- My character has a strong voice and personality that can carry a whole book.
- I'm versatile at using sensory image cues to show my protagonist's feelings rather than flat statements beginning with "I felt ..."
- I'm confident I can still invoke setting details and other character actions in this POV.

Reasons to Choose Second Person

- I want the reader to be as intimate as possible with my character.
- I want my main character to "speak" directly to someone else throughout the novel.
- I have a quirky character with a strong voice or personality who sees the world differently than others.
- I want to convey a wry, witty, or ironic tone in the narrative voice.
- My story thrives on the limited scope of only one character's POV.
- I'm confident I can demonstrate character behavior and not rely too heavily on passive narration.
- I'm confident I can still invoke setting details and other character actions.

Reasons to Choose Third-Person Intimate

- I need to create a balance of intimacy and distance between the reader and my protagonist.
- My story has multiple narrators whose POVs must each be represented.
- I am not as strong at demonstrating character behavior and have a tendency to fall into passive narration.

Reasons to Choose Omniscient

- I need great versatility in moving from the intimate to the distant.
- I need the greatest emotional distance possible.
- I am confident I can make character POV switches without confusing readers.
- My story covers a large span of history or time.
- I need to provide information to the reader that my characters don't or can't know.
- I need to be able to switch between characters' minds within a given scene or chapter.

CHOOSING THE "WRONG" POV

Sometimes the only way to figure out the right POV for your story is to first employ one that doesn't work so well. Many writers have written entire books in one POV and then had to manually change to another (guilty as charged!). While I don't recommend this method, it is sometimes necessary. Switching the POV of an entire novel is deep revision work, because changing the POV forces more than simple pronoun shifts; it alters the access you have to your characters. I once wrote a novel in third-person intimate, but even as I was writing it I felt removed from my character's experience. Switching it to first person allowed me more intimate access.

Personally, I recommend that you test-drive several different POVs and try your hand at different exercises before you write an entire novel. (You can find plenty of exercise in the final chapter in this book.) But if you feel any niggling doubts about the POV you've chosen, rewrite one chapter or scene and see what happens. If the POV switch injects the excerpt with much-needed vitality, then you know it's time for a global change.

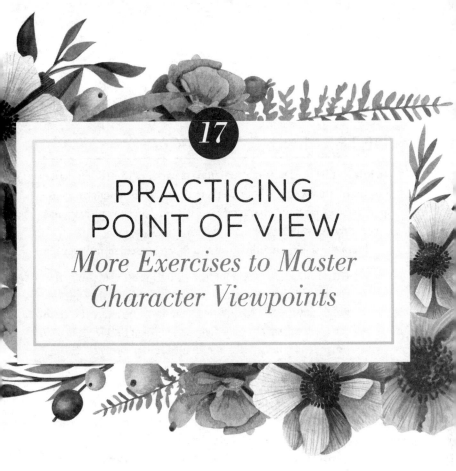

17

PRACTICING POINT OF VIEW
More Exercises to Master Character Viewpoints

"Practice means to perform, over and over again in the face of all obstacles, some act of vision, of faith, of desire. Practice is a means of inviting the perfection desired."

—MARTHA GRAHAM

This chapter is full of exercises that let you explore and play with POV. Even if you think you know which one you'll use for your story, I highly recommend that you experiment first. Fiction is a powerful vehicle to introduce a unique character's experience to readers, to recount situations and events that often don't get enough real-life air time, and to share stories about people whom readers might not have the chance to encounter in their lives. Play with voices and perspectives, intimacy and distance, as you learn to master this crucial element of writing.

DETERMINING THE POV

In this first set of exercises, you'll find six passages from different novels, in different genres. Your challenge for each is to determine the point of view and the character cues within. Check your responses against the Answer Key at the end of this book.

From the science fiction novel *Red Moon* by Benjamin Percy:

> He cannot sleep. All night, even with his eyes closed, Patrick Gamble can see the red numbers of the clock as they click forward: 2:00, 3:30, 4:10, now 4:30, but he is up before the alarm can blare. He snaps on the light and pulls on the blue jeans and black T-shirt folded in a pile, ready for him, ready for this moment, the one he has been dreading for the past two months. His suitcase yawns open on the floor. He tosses his toiletry kit into it after staggering down the hall to the bathroom and rubbing his armpits with a deodorant stick and brushing his teeth, foaming his mouth full of mint toothpaste.
>
> He stands over his suitcase, waiting, as if hoping hard enough would make his hopes come true, waiting until his raised hopes fall, waiting until he senses his father in the bedroom doorway, turning to look at him when he says, "It's time."
>
> He will not cry. His father has taught him that, not to cry, and if he has to, he has to hide it. He zips the suitcase shut and drags it upright and stares at himself in the closet mirror—his jaw stubbled with a few days' worth of whiskers, his eyes so purple with sleeplessness they look like flowers that have wilted in on themselves—before heading down the hall to the living room, where his father is waiting for him.

- What is the POV?
- What are some sensory cues in the excerpt?
- What are some physical-action cues?

- What are some internal-monologue cues?
- What are some imagistic cues?
- What are some dialogue cues?
- What other character reactions are included?

From the surrealist literary novel *In the House upon the Dirt Between the Lake and the Woods* by Matt Bell:

> When her howls subsided, her voice was made different than ever before: There was still some baby inside her, she said, some better other that she might bring forth, and so she worried at the entrance to her womb, first with her fingers and then, later, with tools made for other tasks, until all the bedding was mucked with her. I tried to take these implements from her hands, but with increasing ferocity she shoved me back, with the balls of her freed fists, and with a song that staggered me from the bedside, her new voice climbing, hurling strange my name and the name we had meant for our child. In rising verses, she demanded I disappear, leave her, throw myself into the depths of the salt-soaked lake, cast my now-unwanted bones after the supposed casting of our stillbirth, that failure-son.
>
> Drown yourself away, my wife sang, and then despite my want to stay I found myself again outside the house, for against the fury of her song my horror held neither strength nor will nor strategy.

- What is the POV?
- What are some sensory cues in the excerpt?
- What are some physical-action cues?
- What are some internal-monologue cues?
- What are some imagistic cues?
- What are some dialogue cues?
- What other character reactions are included?

From the short story "Miss Lora" in Junot Díaz's collection *This Is How You Lose Her*:

Always a bikini despite her curvelessness, the top stretching over these corded pectorals and the bottom cupping a rippling fan of haunch muscles. Always swimming underwater, the black waves of her hair flowing behind her like a school of eel. Always tanning herself (which none of the other women did) into the deep lacquered walnut of an old shoe. That woman needs to keep her clothes on, the mothers complained. She's like a plastic bag full of worms. But who could take their eyes off her? Not you or your brother. The kids would ask her, Are you a bodybuilder, Miss Lora? and she would shake her head behind her paperback. Sorry, guys, I was just born this way.

After your brother died, she came over to the apartment a couple of times. She and your mother shared a common place, La Vega, where Miss Lora had been born and where your mother had recuperated after the Guerra Civil. One full year living just behind the Casa Amarilla had made a vegana out of your mother. I still hear the Río Camú in my dreams, your mother said. Miss Lora nodded. I saw Juan Bosch once on our street when I was very young. They sat and talked about it to death. Every now and then she stopped you in the parking lot. How are you doing? How is your mother? And you never knew what to say.

- What is the POV?
- What are some sensory cues in the excerpt?
- What are some physical-action cues?
- What are some internal-monologue cues?
- What are some imagistic cues?
- What are some dialogue cues?
- What other character reactions are included?

From Margaret Atwood's science fiction novel *The Heart Goes Last*:

They held on in their little house, living on fast food and the money from selling the furniture, skimping on energy use and sitting in the dark, hoping things would take an upturn. Finally they put the house on the market, but by then there were no buyers; the houses on either side of theirs were already empty, and the looters had been through them, ripping out anything that could be sold. One day they had no mortgage money left, and their credit cards were frozen. They walked out before they were thrown out, and drove away before the creditors could grab their car.

Luckily Charmaine had saved up a little stash of cash. That, and her tiny pay packet at the bar, plus tips—those have kept them in gas, and a post-office box so they can pretend to have an address if anything does come up for Stan, and the odd trip to the Laundromat when they can't stand the griminess of their clothes.

Stan has sold his blood twice, though he didn't get much for it. "You wouldn't believe it," the woman said to him as she handed him a paper cup of fake juice after his second blood drain, "but some people have asked us if we want to buy their babies' blood, can you imagine?"

- What is the POV?
- What are some sensory cues in the excerpt?
- What are some physical-action cues?
- What are some internal-monologue cues?
- What are some imagistic cues?
- What are some dialogue cues?
- What other character reactions are included?

From Marlon James's literary novel, *A Brief History of Seven Killings*:

One more thing, ostentatious gentlemens. Never turn your back 'pon a white bwoi. After a hot night with no moon all you can think of is that something out to betray you, maybe God, maybe man, but never turn your black 'pon a white bwoi. Turn your back 'pon a white bwoi who drink your mannish water and blush red from the spice and he go back to America and write about how the natives gave him goat's head soup to drink, and the flavor come from blood. Turn your back 'pon a white bwoi when he say he come to the ghetto to look for the Rhythm and he go back to England with your 45s and him get rich while you stay poor. Turn you back 'pon a white bwoi and he will say that is he that shot the

Sherrif, ennit? And make you the deputy then go onstage and say the black wogs and coons and Arabs and f---ing Jamaicans and f---ing blah blah blah don't belong here, we don't want them here …

This was only few weeks ago. Maybe just two. The Singer and the band rehearsing from early morning right into the night. Judy just go call him aside to tell him that that line he singing, *under heavy manners* is a slogan for the PNP and if he sing it that will mean he siding with the PNP, which too many people already suspect …

But he don't say what I also 'fraid to say. … But badness don't mean nothing anymore. Bad can't compete against scheming. Bad can't compete against wicked. I see and a watch them putting me out to pasture, because politics is a new game now and take a different kind of man to play it.

- What is the POV?
- What are some sensory cues in the excerpt?
- What are some physical-action cues?
- What are some internal-monologue cues?
- What are some imagistic cues?
- What are some dialogue cues?
- What other character reactions are included?

From Nathan Filer's novel of psychological suspense, *The Shock of the Fall*:

There is weather and there is climate.

If it rains outside, or if you stab a classmate's shoulder with a compass needle, over and over, until his white cotton school shirt looks like blotting paper, that is the weather.

But if you live in a place where it is often likely to rain, or your perception falters and dislocates so that you retreat, suspicious and afraid of those closest to you, that is the climate.

These are the things we learnt at school.

I have an illness, a disease with a shape and sound of a snake. Whenever I learn something new, it learns it too.

If you have HIV or Cancer, or Athlete's Foot, you can't teach them anything. When Ashley Stone was dying of Meningitis, he might have known that he was dying, but his Meningitis didn't know. Meningitis doesn't know anything. But my illness knows everything that I know. This was a difficult thing to get my head around, but the moment I understood it, my illness understood it too.

These are the things we learnt.
We learnt about atoms.
This illness and me.
I was thirteen.

- What is the POV?
- What are some sensory cues in the excerpt?
- What are some physical-action cues?
- What are some internal-monologue cues?
- What are some imagistic cues?
- What are some dialogue cues?
- What other character reactions are included?

PLAY WITH POINT OF VIEW

For the exercises that follow, either try your hand at writing fresh scenes—which I recommend—or, if you'd rather mix things up in one of the scenes in your manuscript, use one of those. The key here is to play.

We've Got a Problem

Write a scene that introduces your protagonist and his story problem or goal in first person, in the middle of an action—going to an appointment, quitting a job, meeting someone for a first date, etc. Write as much of the scene as you can, using setting, sensory imagery, physical action, and dialogue, and decide on a goal for your character. Leave the scene hanging, unresolved. Avoid using interior monologue.

Now, rewrite the scene in third-person intimate. Have your character think at least one thing he can't say, and put this in italics.

Rewrite the scene in omniscient, and offer one piece of information that the character cannot know.

When you're finished, decide which POV feels most immediate to you, most alive and full of energy. Do you prefer the intimacy of the close POV, or does your story benefit from the distance? How do you offer information to readers that the character can't know? Does this add mystery, or does it feel like authorial intrusion?

Bad News

Write a scene in which one character has to deliver bad news to another character. First write it from the POV of the bad-news deliverer in third-person intimate or omniscient. Then rewrite it from the POV of the bad-news recipient in first person. It's easy to deliver bad news dispassionately but a lot harder to be on the receiving end. Notice which version has more emotional energy.

Stuck in a Rut

Put three characters in a "stuck" spot where emotions tend to run high: a jammed elevator, a ferry on rough waters, a plane experiencing turbulence, etc. Maybe someone has a seizure, or has to urinate so badly she can't hold it, or experiences a mental breakdown. Use omniscience to move into the thoughts of each character during the crisis. Try to reveal one new detail through the mind of each character. Don't forget to also invoke dialogue. Consider, too, how the words of each character reveal emotion and plot detail.

Next, move from external omniscience (all-knowing) into the internal, intimate POV of one of the three characters. Give this character a dilemma: a choice she must make or a confession or a fear to express.

Innocent Until Proven Guilty

Your protagonist is in jail for a crime he did not commit. Imagine the novel is a story told as a letter written to your protagonist's child, in second person, using the "as told to" method. In this scene, your protagonist is recounting the events of the night in question, with the attempt to tell the real truth.

Into the Madding Crowd

Your character is painfully shy, a veteran with PTSD, or suffers from claustrophobia (your choice). Using second-person intimate, put your character into a situation where she has to interact with a large group of people to get an answer that will help her take the next step in her journey. Remember to use sensory cues and physical action cues.

Introduce Yourself

Present a character for the first time to the reader in the following three ways:

- **FIRST PERSON:** Your character is in court with a lawyer, and the judge is reading a list of her "crimes."
- **THIRD-PERSON INTIMATE:** Your character is on a train, and a quirky, eccentric character carrying a battered suitcase and wearing a crazy hat sits in his train compartment. They get into a conversation about where your character is going, and why.
- **OMNISCIENT:** Your character's story is tied to a notable moment in history—marching with Martin Luther King, Jr. for civil rights; in New York City on 9/11; the day the marriage-equality bill passed nationwide. Interweave the omniscient voice to tell readers a few key facts about the historical event, but then drop quickly into a scene and zoom in close to your character. Introduce the character engaged in an action that involves danger. For example, your character could be trampled in a crowd, narrowly escape a burning building, or be besieged by angry protestors.

The Dating Profile

Have your character write a profile in first person that she would post on a dating website (even if she is married).

Social Media

Sum up the key plot points of your character's story in a series of 140-character tweets.

Write five Facebook posts as your character would write them that tell readers about a dramatic experience.

Your character uncovers three Snapchat videos that provide three clues to your plot. Describe them from the POV of the viewer. Then rewrite, describing them from the POV of the character within the videos.

Embody the Other

The following is a list of prompts of characters and situations for you to embody. Use whichever POV feels appropriate, and try to employ imagery, voice, and dialogue—all the cues that best reveal character. Since you won't be doing any research for these, they're just warm-ups. Don't worry so much about getting them "right"; think of the following as practice for entering different kinds of characters. Write:

- a teenager taking her driving exam after a sleepless night
- a young woman beginning her first day of work as the new boss of people twice as old as she
- a young pilot-in-training who must make an emergency flight carrying an injured or ill person
- an indigenous character who has had almost no exposure to outside civilization or technology and who finds an American man unconscious in a canoe, carrying a smart phone
- a Victorian woman in England who takes a risk and breaks a social norm
- a Native American elder who makes a pilgrimage to Washington to plead for the return of his people's sacred land

- an elderly man who wakes up in jail after learning he is responsible for a hit-and-run
- a mother with her baby strapped to her back in an indigenous village raided by Europeans who walks miles through scorching heat to find food
- a deaf character who has to pretend he can hear in order to get a job
- a character living in poverty who wins the lottery
- a preverbal child (You will have to use words, of course, but think as much as you can in purely sensory imagery: sound, color, taste, touch, etc.)
- a character of color in a medical field who must treat a sick or injured racist patient
- a racist, sexist, or xenophobic character who rescues someone who embodies her own hatred and prejudice (These types of scenes can be tough to write, but sometimes it's worth a shot.)
- a celebrity with agoraphobia who must appear at a press conference

AFTERWORD

By now I hope this book has pulled back the curtain on point of view and made it less mysterious. What I most want to imprint on you is that *how* you tell your story is intimately linked to *who* is telling it. The storytelling style must be woven from the threads of your character's inner life and world. Unless you're writing memoir, *you* are never actually telling the story. That's a strange concept, I know, because those words don't magically appear on the page—they are put there by your hand.

It might help to think of your prose writing in terms of screen- or playwriting. In a script, the writer provides physical action and dialogue cues to characters to act out on a stage or set. The major difference in prose is that you also have to find a way to fill in all the information in between—all that emotion, thought, and narrative voice we've discussed—in a way that doesn't sound like *you* but rather like the characters. In a way, storytelling *is* a kind of magic: In speaking through your characters, you give them life and, at the same time, fade into the background.

I encourage you to try as many of the exercises in this book as possible, because, like any form of strength training, they will flex new muscles of writing craft that you may never have used before and push you to consider points of view that stretch your skills and widen your experience. When in doubt, stick to the simplest forms of POV, as limited and internal as you can get, to pull your reader intimately close and offer a literary embrace that will keep them turning pages.

INDEX

Writing the Intimate Character

Index

Writing the Intimate Character

ANSWER KEY

From the science fiction novel *Red Moon* by Benjamin Percy:
A: Third-person intimate

From the surrealist literary novel *In the House upon the Dirt Between the Lake and the Woods* by Matt Bell:
A: First person

From the short story "Miss Lora" in Junot Díaz's collection *This Is How You Lose Her*:
A: Second person, "as told to" method; the narrator is addressing another person.

From Margaret Atwood's science fiction novel *The Heart Goes Last*:
A: Omniscient; the POV moves between internal (what the character knows) and external (what the character can't know).

From Marlon James's literary novel, *A Brief History of Seven Killings*:
A: Trick paragraph—this excerpt starts out in the second-person universal and then drifts into what seems like omniscience, until we realize it's all being dictated in first person.

From Nathan Filer's novel of psychological suspense, *The Shock of the Fall*:
A: The excerpt starts out in the second-person universal and then transitions to first person.